The Charleston Ballet

LANGUAGE OF DANCE SERIES

Editor

Ann Hutchinson Guest

Director, Language of Dance Centre, London, UK

No. 1:

The Flower Festival in Genzano Pas de Deux

by Ann Hutchinson Guest

No. 2:

Fundamentals of Dance

by Ted Shawn

by Ann Hutchinson Guest

No. 3:

Nijinsky's Faune Restored

by Ann Hutchinson Guest
and Claudia Jeschke

No. 4:

Tudor's *Soirée Musicale*

by Ann Hutchinson Guest

No. 5:

Ballade by Anna Sokolow

Compiled by Ray Cook

Edited by Ann Hutchinson Guest

No. 6:

La Vivandière Pas de Six

by Ann Hutchinson Guest

No. 7:

Robert le Diable

The Ballet of the Nuns

By Knud Arne Jürgensen
and Ann Hutchinson Guest

No. 8:

The Green Table

Text written and compiled
by Anna Markard

Edited by Ann Hutchinson Guest

No. 9:

Jerome Robbins' *The Charleston Ballet* by Ann Hutchinson Guest

The Charleston Ballet

CHOREOGRAPHY BY

JEROME ROBBINS

MUSIC BY

MORTON GOULD

DANCE NOTATION SCORE BY

ANN HUTCHINSON GUEST

THE NOVERRE PRESS

Copyright © 2019 by Ann Hutchinson Guest

Choreography copyright © 1946 by Jerome Robbins

Charleston
Composed by Morton Gould
© 1945 Chappell & Co Inc
Warner Chappell North America Ltd, London, W8 5DA
Reproduced by permission of Faber Music Ltd
All Rights Reserved.

First published in 2019 by The Noverre Press

The Noverre Press
Southwold House
Isington Road
Binsted
Hampshire
GU34 4PH

A CIP catalogue record for this book is available from the British Library

ISBN: 978-1-906830-86-1

Permission for public performance of this work must be obtained in writing from Christopher Pennington of the Jerome Robbins Foundation in New York City.

No part of this book may be reproduced or utilised in any form or by any means, electronic or mechanical, including photocopying and recording, or by any information storage or retrieval system, without permission in writing from the publishers.

DEDICATION

To my late husband, Ivor Guest

(strange term 'late', he was never late)

for all your support and understanding that

made it possible for me to publish choreographic works.

This one is especially dedicated to you.

HOWEVER

I also dedicate this book to

Jerome Robbins,

The most gifted choreographer I have ever known.

What a privilege it was to have worked with you

and experienced your constant, rich

outpouring of movement ideas.

CONTENTS

Introduction to the Series	8
Acknowledgements	9
Billion Dollar Baby – the 1945 Broadway Musical	10
The Plot of the Broadway Show	10
Dance Scenes	11
Jerome Robbins and Morton Gould – Biographical Notes	12
The Charleston Ballet	14
The Original Cast	14
Set and costumes	14
The Plot of the Charleston Ballet	15
Notating the Charleston Ballet	16
Working with Robbins	16
List of Characters	18
The Video Recording	18
The Dance Score	19
The Music Score	79
Pictures of specific moments in the ballet	99

INTRODUCTION TO THE SERIES

The *Language of Dance Series* aims to expand the literature of dance through publication of key works that cover a range of dance styles and dance periods.

A language is spoken, written and read. Those intimately involved in the study and performance of dance will have experienced the language of dance in its 'spoken' form, i.e. when it is danced. During the years spent in mastering dance, the component parts are discovered and become part of one's dance language. Through its written form these component parts, the 'building blocks' common to all forms of dance become clear, as well as how these blocks are used. The study of the Language of Dance incorporates these basic elements and the way they are put together to produce choreographic sentences. How the movement sequences are performed, the manner of 'uttering' them, rests on the individual's interpretation.

Through careful study of appropriate movement description, these gems of dance heritage have been translated into Labanotation, the highly developed method of analysing and recording movement.

In the *Language of Dance Series* understanding of the material is enriched through study and performance notes, which provide an aid in exploring the movement sequences and bringing the choreography to life. Whenever possible there is included historical background to place the work in context, as well as additional information of value to researchers and dance scholars.

Dr. Ann Hutchinson Guest, Editor

ACKNOWLEDGEMENTS

The Charleston Book

As 2018 was Jerome Robbins' centenary year, I decided to honour him by publishing the dance score of his Charleston Ballet from the 1945 Broadway musical *Billion Dollar Baby*, thereby making this valuable choreographic gem available to the dance world.

In New York Chris Pennington of the Jerome Robbins Foundation gave me permision to publish this ballet and kindly provided links to the other people I needed to see. Linda Murray, director of the New York Public Library Dance Collection, and Phil Karg, arranged for me to see the 1988 film of me, score in hand, rehearsing the Charleston choreography with two quick-learning lead dancers in preparation for the show *Jerome Robbins' Broadway*. With their aides, Linda and Phil also searched the Dance Collection files for photos of the Charleston Ballet, alas that only a few could be found. Linda also introduced me to Rebecca Paller at the Paley Center for Media. When I visited, the section which featured the Charleston ballet from the 1953 Ford Motor Company's 50th Anniversary Celebration film had already been selected. This recording is the most faithful because not only was my score used, but also many members of the original cast in the 1945 *Billion Dollar Baby* show were again dancing their roles including me as the Timid Girl. I was put in touch with Carol Kogan who is in charge of rights and permissions for Films Around the World. I was given a DVD copy of the Charleston for my personal use. For the sheet music included in the book I am grateful to Morton Gould, the composer, who years ago had given me a copy of the music reduction. To obtain the needed official permission to publish the sheet music that Morton Gould had given me, I embarked on a three-month search during which the following people were especially helpful: his daughter, Abby Gould Burton, Sargent Aborn of TamsWitmark and finally Charlotte Mortimer of Faber Music in London who had the official right to conclude my quest; to each of them I extend much appreciation for their help.

Most importantly, I am greatly indebted to Andy Adamson who undertook to put the Labanotation score into the computer using the Calaban system he had developed at Birmingham University. His general comments and many suggestions have been most valuable.

Julie Brodie, of the Dance Department at Kenyon College in Gambier, Ohio, undertook the task of reviving the Charleston Ballet for performance from the Labanotation score, thus giving the notation this invaluable proofreading test. For her eagle eye and painstaking work I am indeed grateful.

For his computer skills and ability to sort out the various photos, permissions and credit lines, I am greatly indebted to my colleague Raymundo Ruiz.

BILLION DOLLAR BABY – the 1945 Broadway Musical

Produced by Paul Feigay and Oliver Smith, with book and lyrics written by Betty Comden and Adolph Green and music by Morton Gould, *Billion Dollar Baby* was choreographed by Jerome Robbins, directed by George Abbot and had costumes designed by Irene Sharaff. It was a story of gangsters and flappers in the 1920s Prohibition era and included a bathing beauty contest, a gangster's funeral and a dance marathon.

Billion Dollar Baby opened at the Alvin Theater on 21 December 1945 and closed 29 June 1946 after 220 performances. The era of the 1920s was perhaps, in 1945, a bit too recent, interest in it developed only a decade or so later. As a result the show did not have the success it deserved.

The Alvin Theater marquee.

Jerome Robbins © The Robbins Rights Trust.

The Plot of the Broadway Show

The plot of *Billion Dollar Baby* involved a millionaire, M. M. Montague, played by Robert Chisholm, and his girlfriend, played by Mitzi Green (who had a couple of "show biz" songs, reminiscent of Texas Guinan). Joan McCracken, a lovely ballet dancer who had made her name in the Catherine Littlefield Ballet, was the leading gold-digging character Maribelle Jones, a Sweet Young Thing on a quest for wealth in the Prohibition Era. Danny Daniels, an accomplished tap dancer, played her faithful boyfriend in the play. Maribelle, after joining up with the leading gangster, sets her sights on the millionaire. The complex story included a gangster's funeral and an Atlantic City bathing beauty contest, with the singers being Miss Montana, Miss Arizona, etc. There was also a take-off of *The Zeigfeld Follies,* with the singers as elegant showgirls, parading around in fishnet stockings, feathers – the lot, two of them being perched high on swings. All were singing;

"A lovely girl is like a lovely bird"

An obvious take-off of "A lovely girl is like a melody". This luscious scene was interrupted by a gangster shoot-out, leaving the screaming singers as frightened crumpled lumps – a fitting end to the first Act.

In the second act there was the Dance Marathon number, in which each couple had to feign increasing exhaustion, carrying on by the skin of their teeth, gradually dropping one after the other, and being dragged off by the attendants (the male singers who also doubled at times as gangsters). The winning couple was, of course, Danny Daniels and Joan McCracken. As he was a very fine tap dancer (he later choreographed and performed Morton Gould's Tap Dance Concerto), Danny had to have a featured number. This was achieved (rather implausibly after being on the edge of exhaustion) by a sudden burst of energy enabling him to perform a very complex dance involving intricate foot work and drumstick rhythms as he whirled and tapped his way around a big drum, a drum that somehow managed to arrive at centre stage just when needed! But he was so good that none of this illogicality mattered.

Dance Scenes

Another significant second act scene was in a bar. Two of the dancers, Lorraine Todd and Joan Mann, were ladies of easy virtue, dressed in what was then very daring, but is now seen in the street: red tank tops and tight shiny red elastic 'pants', coming to halfway down the thigh. Such revealing of the crotch and curves of the bottom was new, but right for that scene. A few gangsters came

Jerome Robbins with Leonard Bernstein
and Oliver Smith, 1944, *Life Magazine*
© NYPL

in and the easy friendship developed into the sex act. Robbins kept the choreography suggestive but sufficiently stylised to be 'tasteful'. Lorraine Todd, who was very well suited to the show, had nearly been dropped after the first two days of rehearsal. She was small, obviously an experienced show dancer, and quite sophisticated with her hair pinned up with curls on top, as was then the style. Robbins was uncertain about keeping her, but on the third day when she came in with her hair down, Robbins saw an entirely different person in her and, as a result, used her effectively. She was one of the flappers in the Charleston Ballet, the other two being Helen Gallagher and Virginia Gorski, both of whom went on to bigger and better roles in show business.

Billion Dollar Baby was ahead of its time. Because interest in the '20s and reversion to the fashions and hair styles of that period only arrived several years later, the show did not have the success it deserved. Several of the women in the cast were reluctant to have their hair cut short. Joan McCracken eased into it with a sparse fringe to start with and then full 'bangs' when she realised how attractive she looked. Some cut short sides, brushing them forward, and arranged the back hair in a net to make it appear short.

Jerome Robbins – Biographical Note

I would like to give a somewhat personal account of Robbins career. He first came to my attention in a Ballets Russe performance of *Capriccio Espagnol* in which he made such a dynamic entrance that I thought he was Leonide Massine. In all his performances he displayed a sensitive awareness of dynamic changes in movement.

Jerome Robbins (11 October 1918 – 29 July 1998) was a renowned American dancer, director, producer and choreographer who worked extensively in classical ballet, on Broadway and in film and television. In his lifetime, Robbins won five Tony Awards, two Academy Awards and was a recipient of the Kennedy Center Honors.

In 1944 he created and performed in *Fancy Free,* a ballet about sailors on leave. Later that year he launched his Broadway career with the musical *On The Town,* inspired by the success of *Fancy Free.* Leonard Bernstein wrote the music and Oliver Smith designed the sets. The book and lyrics were by a team that Robbins would work with again, Betty Comden and Adolph Green, and the director was the Broadway legend George Abbott. The next year, in 1945, he was involved in the jazz age musical *Billion Dollar Baby* in which the Charleston Ballet was featured. In 1947 he received acclaim for his humorous "Mack Sennett" ballet in *High Button Shoes* for which he won his first Tony Award for choreography. While forging his career on Broadway, Robbins continued to work in ballet as a performer but mostly as a choreographer, creating works such as *Interplay* and *Facsimile.* In 1949 he joined George Balanchine and Lincoln Kirstein as Associate Artistic Director for the newly-formed New York City Ballet. He choreographed *Age of Anxiety, The Cage, Afternoon of a Faun,* and *The Concert.* On Broadway he created dances for *Call Me Madam* and – notably, for *The King and I* in which he created the celebrated *Small House of Uncle Thomas* ballet. He also choreographed *The Pyjama Game, Gypsy* and *Fiddler on the Roof.* An outstanding

Jerome Robbins.   Morton Gould.

Jesse Gerstein © The Robbins Rights Trust.   Photo courtesy of Abby Burton.

achievement was his conception of *West Side Story,* a contemporary version of *Romeo and Juliet* with music by Leonard Bernstein.

Morton Gould – Biographical Note

Morton Gould (10 December 1913 – 21 February 1996) was an American composer, conductor, arranger, and pianist. At six, he had his first composition published ("Just Six"), and thereafter played in concerts until age 17. He was educated at New York University and was a music student of Abby Whiteside and Vincent Jones. His long and fruitful career did much to erase the lines between concert and popular idioms. He was a prolific and versatile composer whose works reflected the moods and outlook of his country in all its rough-and-tumble optimism.

On a personal note: during the boring all-night setting of the lighting for the *Billion Dollar Baby* show, Morton thought of the dancers and brought us some whisky to cheer us up. When the show closed he gave each of the female dancers a beautiful silk scarf, I have mine still.

THE CHARLESTON BALLET

The Original Cast

Policeman……………………….	Arthur Partington
Three Flappers…………….……	Loraine Todd, Helen Gallagher, Virginia Gorski
Rich Couple……………………..	Joan Mann, Fred Hearne
Timid Girl……………………….	Ann Hutchinson
Good-Time-Charlie……………..…	Billy Skipper
Collegiate Couple………………..	Virginia Poe, Doug Deane
Two Gangsters……………….….	Lucas Arco, Allen Waine
Younger Generation Couple………	Maria Harriton, Bill Summer
Old Couple………………………..	Jacquie Dodge, Joe Landis

Extras: Man at Speakeasy door to open the sliding panel and the door. Two Bootleggers (neither of whom dance) played by singers.

Set and Costumes

The set is a street scene in New York City in the Twenties with an entrance to a Speakeasy. In the show the dance was performed in "two" i.e. two wings in depth, hence the narrowness of the stage plans. Each person revealed their character through a particular manner of performing Robbins' carefully chosen variations on the Charleston vocabulary. The costumes by Irene Sharaff were an exaggeration of the period. Hair styles and make-up clearly had to echo that era. Some of the cast disliked having to cut their hair short, in my case it was left long and I had a permanent wave to make it a bit frizzy. Other than in the Charleston ballet, I wore my hair with swirls over the ears, in "Cootie Garage" style (a cootie being World War I slang for a nit).

The three flappers wore cloche hats with a big bobble, their dresses had mid-thigh length pleated skirts, no waistline and a flat top. The rich man was in evening dress with a top hat, his lady in a slinky evening dress, with a fur piece coat and long cigarette holder. As the Timid Girl I wore a grey-green dress covered in layers of fringe, and a cloche hat with long curved feathers extending forward from below my ears. The Collegiate Couple had 'raccoon' coats made out of woolly blobs. Each had a hat. The gangsters were in black suits and bowler hats. The Younger Generation banjo-player and his gal wore slicker rain coats, they also had hats. The Old Couple wore unfashionable clothes and hats.

The Plot of the Charleston Ballet

A policeman enters, sauntering nonchalantly across the stage. As he exits, three flappers come in and take over, going through their various antics, their favourite Charleston movements, poses and expressions: "Whoopee!", "Hotcha!", etc. As they exit, the rich couple enters with their stilted, snooty manner. He knocks on the speakeasy door, presents a card, takes his lady's coat before they are both admitted.

The Timid Girl, (she lives alone in an attic) soulfully enters minding her own business. Stooped and pathetic-looking, fringes 'jiggling', she turns her head to look at the audience with a blank gaze. Bumping into Good Time Charlie by the speakeasy door, they embark on a swift pantomime sequence – tricky to keep the basic Charleston step going while rapidly miming the conversation. She: "Oh! How you startled me!" "Come and have a drink." "Who, me in there? Never!" "Aw, cummon!" "Well, er…." A collegiate couple in raccoon coats, brandishing a flask of whiskey, burst out of the Speakeasy. They frolic and imbibe in front of the Timid Girl and Good-Time-Charlie. After cavorting around, sharing the flask, she jumps on his back and they exit stage right. The Timid Girl starts to follow them but Charlie grabs her wrist, she resists but he unceremoniously drags her into the speakeasy.

Two gangsters now enter, "casing the joint", is the coast clear? The policeman enters briefly, salutes the gangsters who go ahead, beckoning to two men delivering the crates of whisky into the speakeasy. The three flappers now come in and take up with the gangsters but each walks off in a huff, in turn saying, "Mind your own beeswax", "Don't be an Airedale", and "So's your Aunt Tillie". The gangsters then enter the Speakeasy.

A Younger Generation banjo-player in a slicker enters from stage left, soon followed by his mate. As he strums the banjo, she beats time. He stops and says "You are the cat's pyjamas!" They exit stage right as the Old Couple comes in. These oldsters gingerly perform the various Charleston steps. He slaps her bottom and says "You're a red hot mamma!" Seeing that no one is looking, they sneak into the Speakeasy. Once more the policeman makes his rounds, crossing the stage and passing the juvenile as he enters stage right. The first flapper enters from stage right, but soon exits travelling backward into the wing.

Suddenly the Speakeasy door bursts open, out roll the two gangsters and Good Time Charlie pushed out by the Timid Girl. Hat gone, hair all wild, high as a kite she stands there oblivious to the Tahitian-style pelvic rotations which had taken hold of her nether region. Gradually becoming aware of the pelvic activity, to stop it, she grabs her thighs, pulling her knees together and screams. She then breaks into a frenzied Lindy-like Charleston the men egging her on. This sequence leads into the finale, all couples coming back on stage. The gangsters each take a Flapper, the third Flapper has the banjo and strums it in the right downstage corner. This last section was Robbins in full spate, involving as it did a most exhausting series of lifts, plus "wheelbarrow" runs, both backward and then forward criss-crossing the stage. The other couples enter and during the 'Windmill step' the first flapper crosses through them, playing the banjo, and exits. Unison movement for the couples now follows. The climax of dancing, interrupted by "Does she pet?" "You bet!" is then followed by utter exhaustion where everyone spins around and limply falls to the floor. All just breathe with knees bouncing. A sudden burst of energy leg kick here, a sudden "Hotcha!" or a weak "Whoopee!" while the policeman passes through them as he crosses the stage. All slowly pick themselves up off the ground and exit into the Speakeasy. The Timid Girl and Good Time Charlie are the last, pausing by the Speakeasy door to take a moment to say thank you. As she says goodbye, she travels backward into the wing while he enters the Speakeasy. All having exited, there is a moment before they all rush back in for a 'flash' finish, everyone takes up a characteristic pose. A 'show biz' ending that Robbins felt was necessary. For this pose the Timid girl has her hat on, it having been handed to her in the wing before she rushed onstage again.

Notating the Charleston Ballet

Two weeks before *Billion Dollar Baby* closed in July 1946, I decided this gem of a work should not be lost, so I wrote down all of my part in Labanotation, getting the different counts and sequences from the other dancers. With this score in hand, it was possible to reproduce the work faithfully. In 1953 my score was referred to when Robbins rehearsed the piece for the Ford Motor Company's 50th Anniversary extravaganza. Robbins called on my assistance again in 1988 for his epic *Jerome Robbins' Broadway*, for which many of his best Broadway numbers were revived. None went quicker in rehearsal than the Charleston Ballet because time was not wasted in trying to remember the steps and floor plans. During two days of rehearsing, I, with my dance score in hand, taught each part to two very accomplished show dancers. They were incredible, but inevitably, with the time gap between my teaching the material and their teaching it to the new cast weeks later, there was loss of detail, such as the timing, the mime gestures and other special Robbins effects. Also 'watered down' were the costumes. The fringed dress for the Timid Girl originally had rows of fringe from top to bottom; the new costume had fringe only on the skirt – not the same effect. Unfortunately it is this somewhat inferior version that is available on YouTube.

New York City Ballet rehearsal of *Dances at a Gathering* with Allegra Kent and Jerome Robbins, choreography by Jerome Robbins (New York) 1969. Martha Swope © NYPL

Working with Robbins

Working with Robbins (or 'Jerry' as we called him) was a marvellous experience, but not without its frustrations. Never before nor since have I experienced a choreographer so brimming over with ideas. He would toss off one movement after another, rapidly discarding something if our reaction to it, our "taking it over," did not please him. And Robbins was not easily pleased. He expected full performance level by the third time you tried out a new movement; no gentle easing into it, no gradual finding one's way and identifying with the movement. As the dancers respected Robbins enormously, we knocked ourselves out to please him. This was not easy, as negative comments came easily to him, and words of praise or appreciation were non-existent or extremely rare. I realised much later the tremendous pressure he was under; he had a reputation to maintain and a career to continue to forge. But it was hard to accept some of his behaviour in rehearsals. After mapping out a sequence one day he would look at it the next day and say, "What are you doing? I never gave you those movements!" We would gulp, look at each other and carry on, knowing darned well he had. There was a definite love/hate relationship toward Robbins on the part of the dancers. It was during rehearsals for this show that an incident happened which became a part of Robbins – and Broadway – lore. Robbins, ranting at the dancers on stage, gradually moved backward. The Alvin stage had no footlights; as he got close to the orchestra pit, we all froze, not one of us could bring ourselves to call out a warning word "Watch it, Jerry!" He fell in – fortunately he was wearing his winter coat and only his ego was hurt.

My request to Jerry to use my Charleston score in the classroom for educational purposes was consistently refused: "I don't want untrained bodies doing my movements!" he stated. Fortunately other choreographers have more vision and more concern for the education of future dancers and trainee choreographers. When he was in the mood, Robbins could be delightful. I was in Copenhagen when he taught his ballet *Fanfare* to the Danish Ballet. We were in the airport together as we were leaving, and he couldn't have been nicer. I did have a chance some time later when he agreed to have coffee, to ask if he would consider choreographing a balletic piece that teenage students could perform, i.e. not too difficult. I would notate it and then it would be available to future generations of students. He turned it down, saying "If I am going to spend that kind of time I might as well do a proper piece with professionals and get paid."

Jerome Robbins and Mikhail Baryshnikov rehearsing *Other Dances*, no. 379, 1976. Martha Swope © NYPL

Allegra Kent and Jerome Robbins rehearsing his ballet, *Dances at a Gathering*, 1969, Martha Swope © NYPL

List of Characters

A	Policeman
B	A Flapper
C	A Flapper
D	A Flapper
E	Rich Lady
F	Rich Man
G	Timid Girl
H	Good Time Charlie
J	Collegiate Boy
K	Collegiate Girl
L	A Gangster
M	A Gangster
N	Younger Generation Boy
O	Younger Generation Girl
P	Old Lady
Q	Old Man

The Video Recording

To access the video recording of the 1953 Ford Motor Company's 50th anniversary celebration for which the Charleston Ballet was performed, go to the following website address for the YouTube link to the "Ford 50th Anniversary Show":

https://www.youtube.com/watch?v=XcHCluMpZBU

At about 56 minutes into the programme you will find the start of the Charleston Ballet. This version is the best since almost all the dancers had been in the 1956 Broadway Show *Billion Dollar Baby*. However, not so welcome in this recording is the lack of the entrance for the Flappers, and the absence of the stilted entrance of the Rich Couple. The fancy camera shots during the energetic group dancing, all make the choreography less easy to follow. In the Broadway show the concluding pose for the dancers was spread across the stage; in the Ford production the dancers ended in a close group.

The video of the Charleston Ballet as revived for the "Jerome Robbins Broadway" production lacks a great deal of detail needed for fully understanding the gestures and the telling of the story.

THE DANCE SCORE
Glossary

Parts of the Body

| Mouth | Eyes | Right Eye | Tongue | Top of Head | Forehead | Nose |

Travelling

= A short distance (Meas. 61, 63 E,F)

= Direction modified (B, m.55)

= See floor plan (B, m.55)

Shifting Body Part

= Shift head forward (Q, meas. 190)

= Shift pelvis to side (N, meas. 165)

= Shift pelvis forward (P, meas. 192)

Relationships - the Meeting Line

B = B is in front of you (L, meas. 152)

L = L is in front of you (B, meas. 152)

L / M = L is above M (L, meas. 138)

Cancellation

∧ = result of previous indication disappears (i.e. back to normal)

Contact Bows

= Arms touching torso (B,C,D, meas.12)

When two body parts are linked with a vertical bow it indicates contact, touch. (B,C,D meas. 14)

A double vertical bow = sliding

(B,C,D, meas. 148) (licking the thumb)

Relating

⇑——A
L

L's right arm addresses A (m. 141)

⇑
J
K

K passes under J's left arm (m. 98)

Accent Sign

A large accent sign refers to the whole movement: ❱
(G, m. 88)

Gathering Sign

∫
⇑
= beckoning the bootleggers in (L, meas. 137)

Specific Timing

For meas. 61-64 the notation has been kept simple, but the performers should follow their instinct by stepping on the off-beat accented notes in the music. There is an automatic tendency to do so.

Words in the Score

Note that words written in quotation marks are actually spoken (B,C,D m.46)
Words in brackets are there to give additional clarity to the intention of movement (B,C,D m.51)

Ad lib Signs

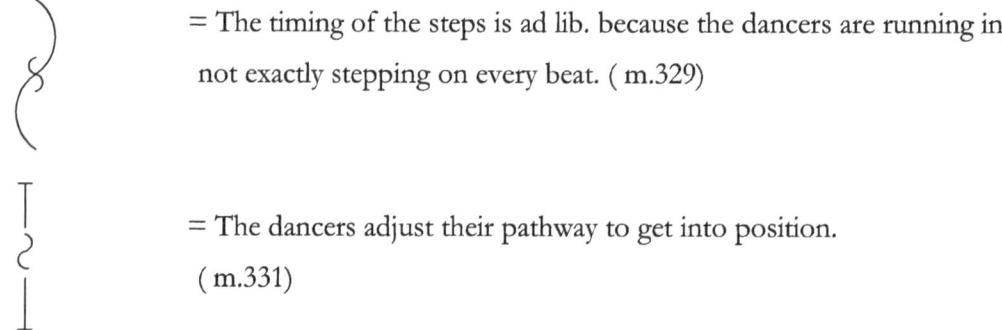

= The timing of the steps is ad lib. because the dancers are running in, not exactly stepping on every beat. (m.329)

= The dancers adjust their pathway to get into position. (m.331)

THE DANCE SCORE 21

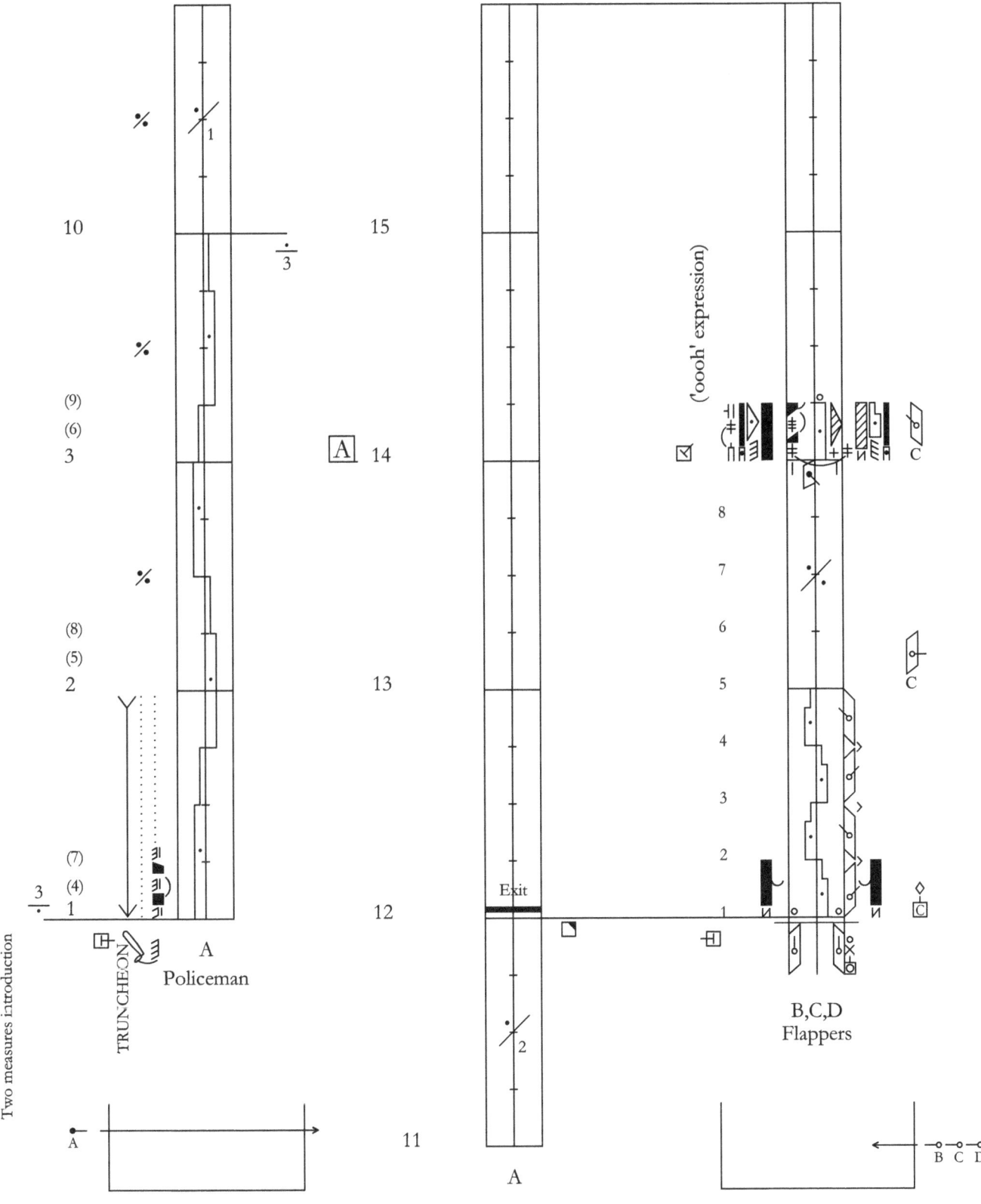

22 THE CHARLESTON BALLET

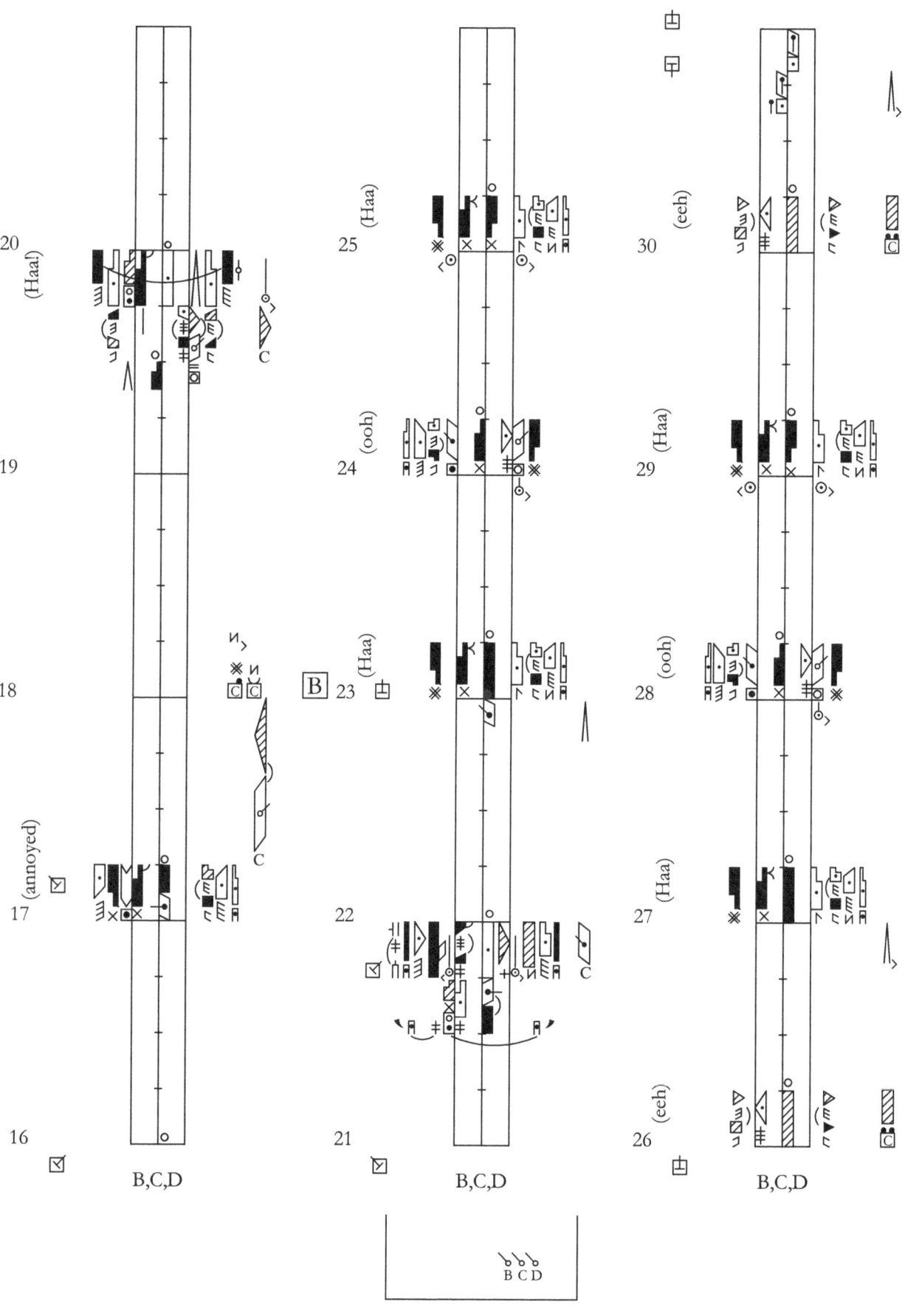

meas. 17

THE DANCE SCORE

23

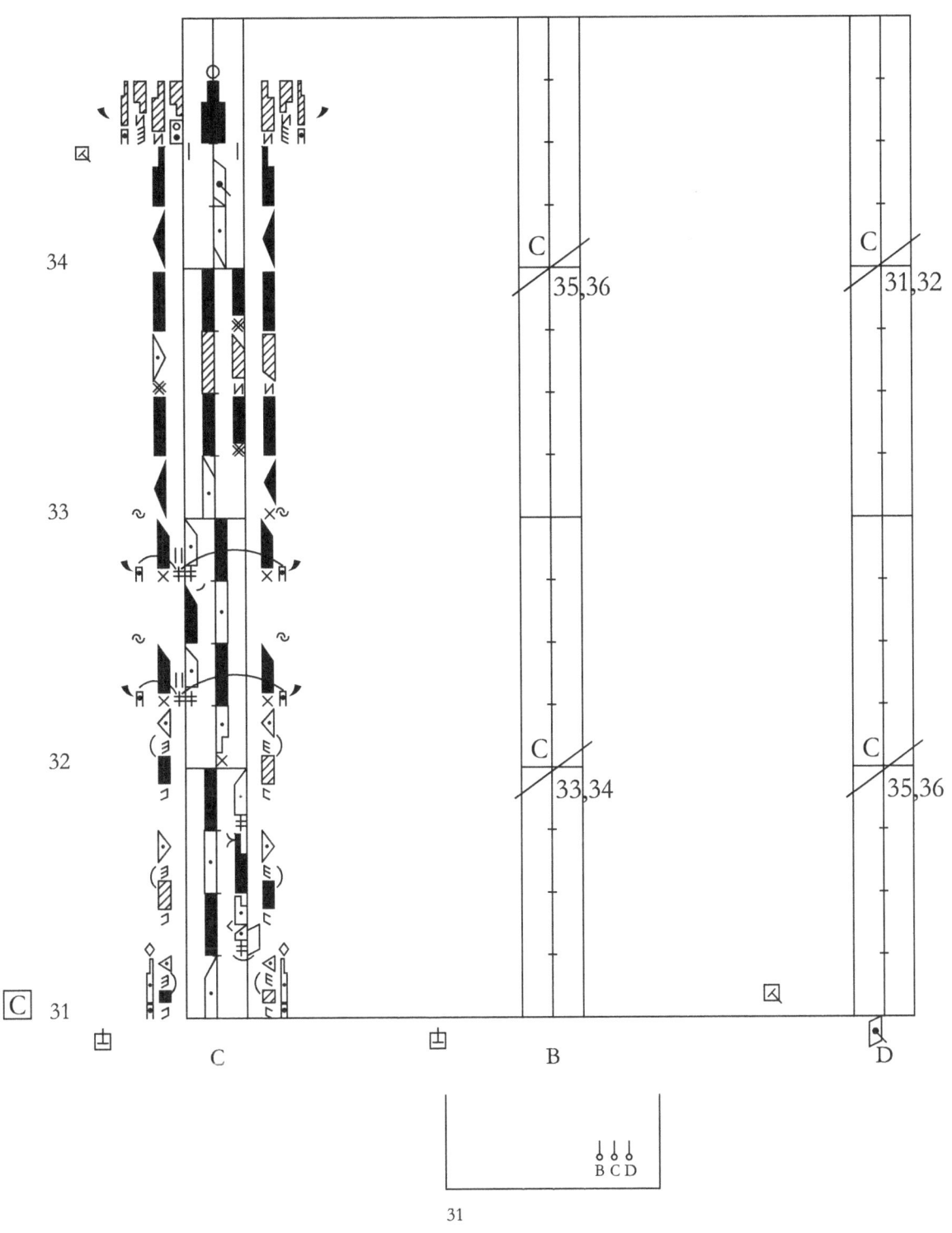

24 THE CHARLESTON BALLET

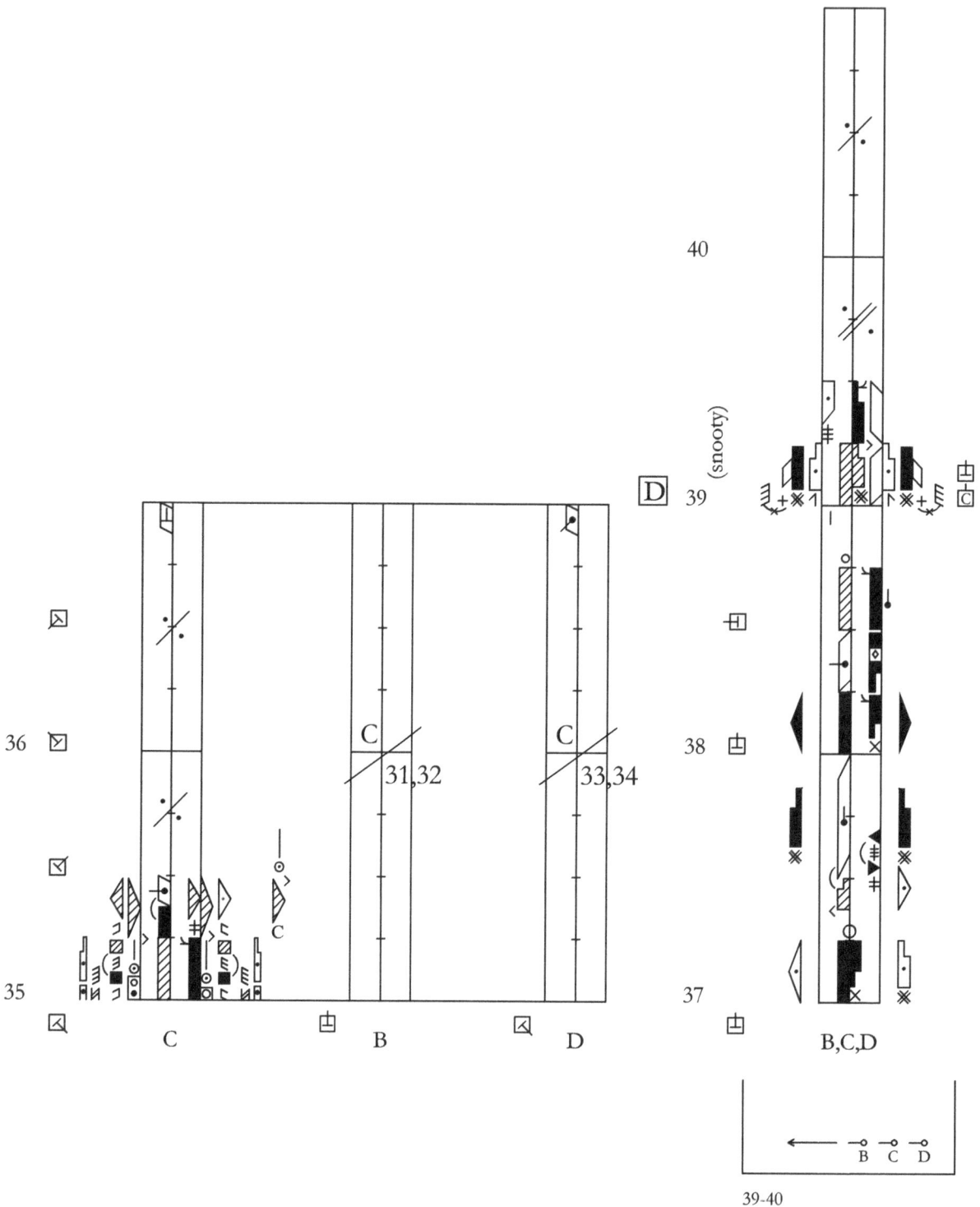

THE DANCE SCORE

25

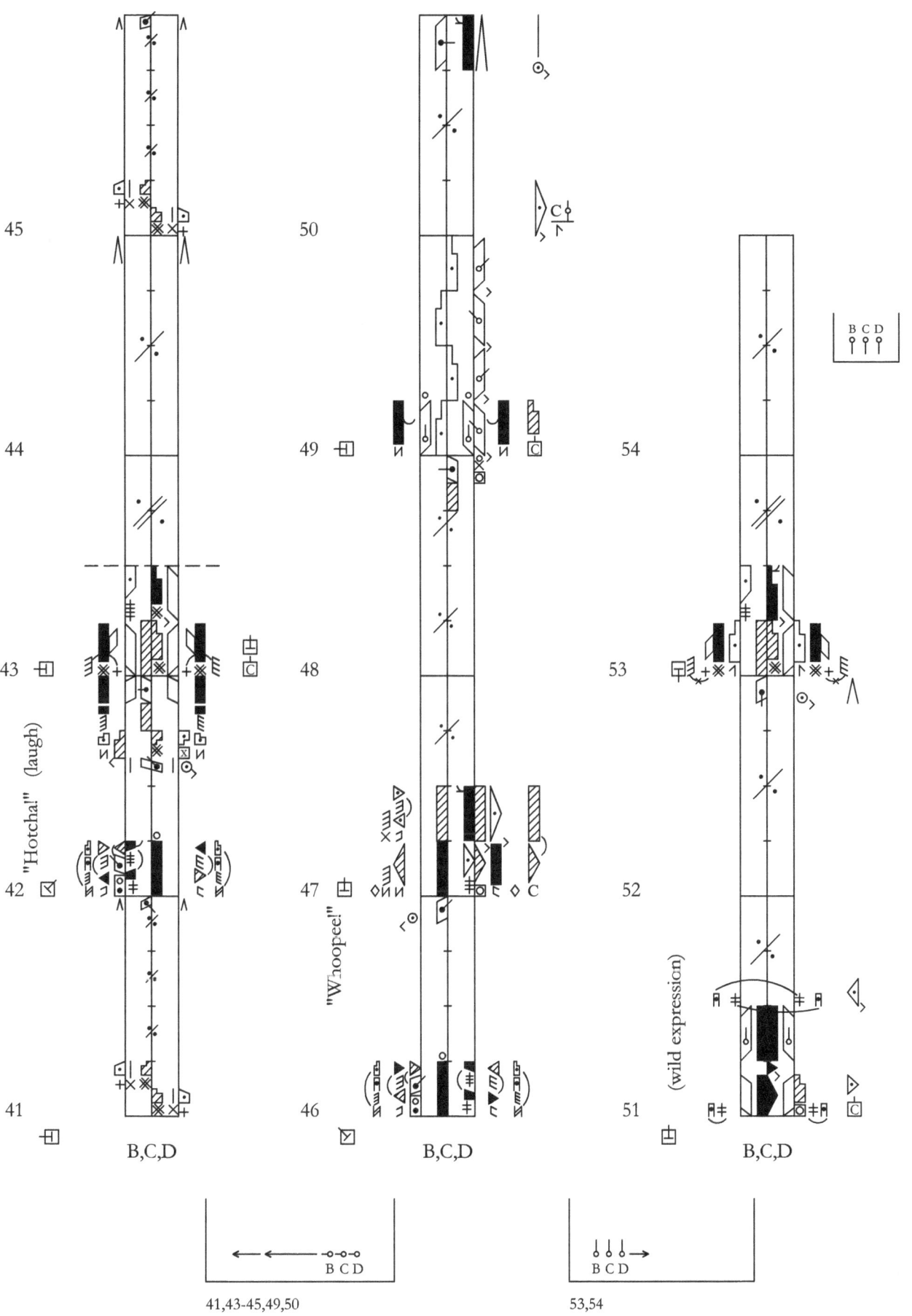

26 THE CHARLESTON BALLET

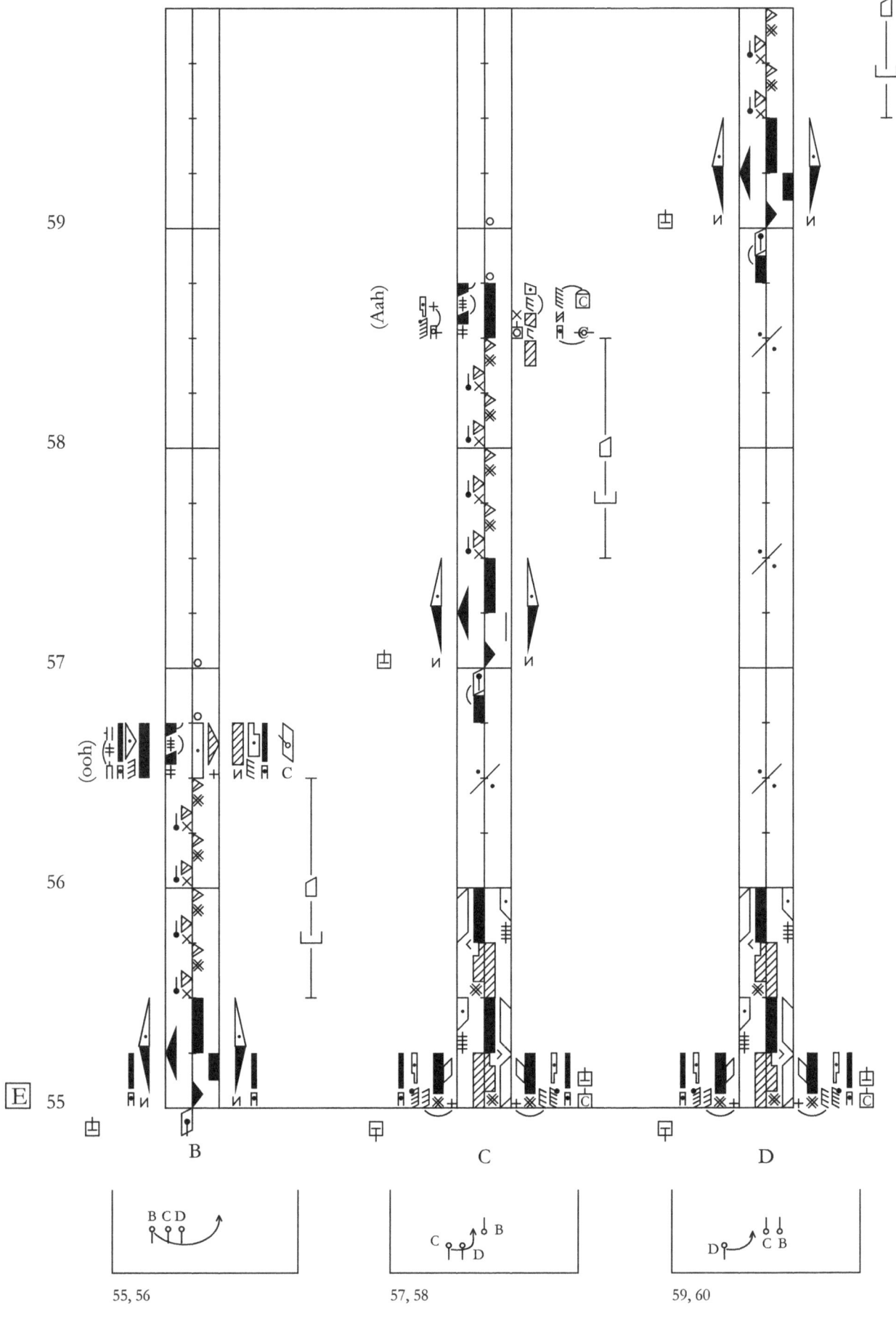

THE DANCE SCORE 27

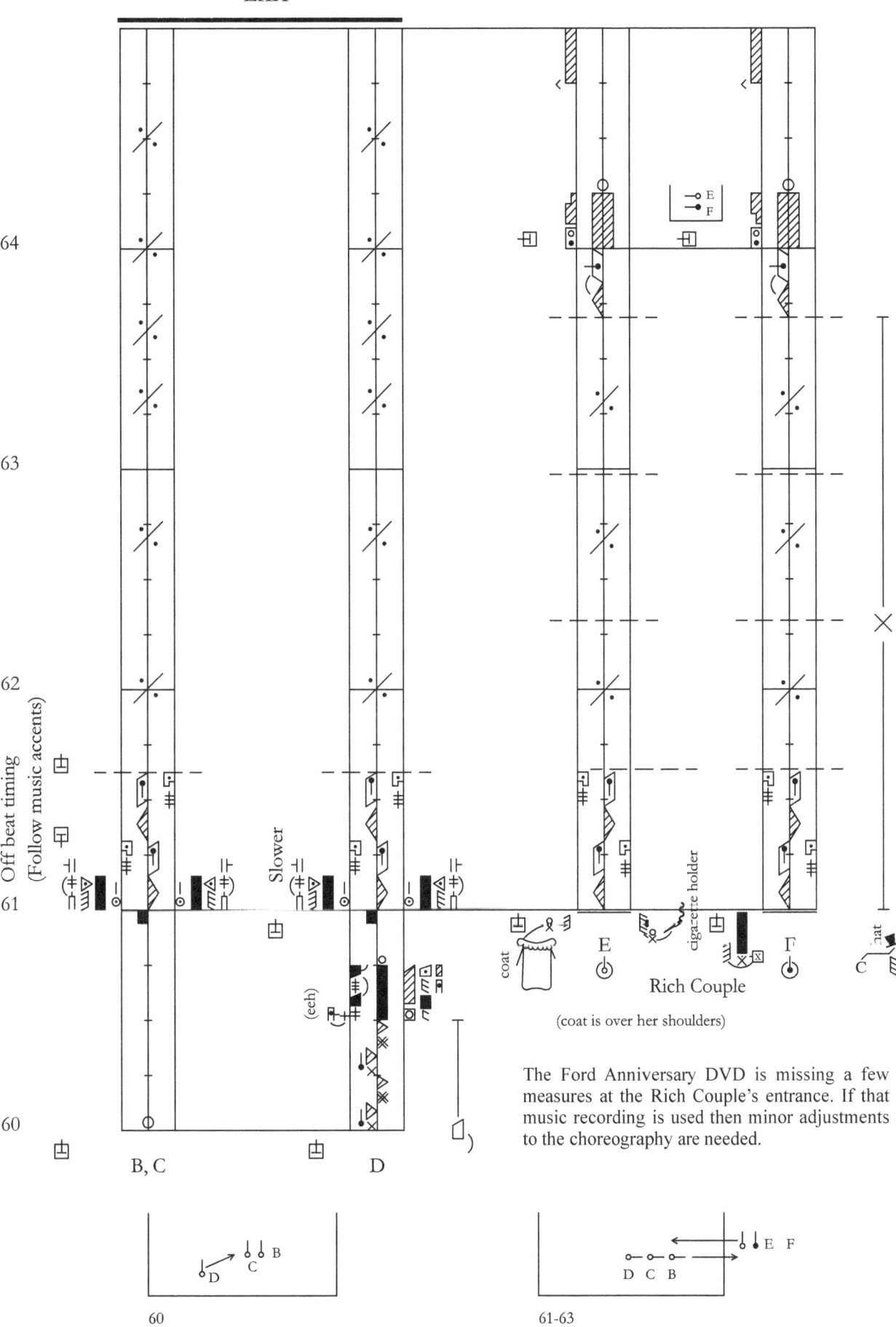

28 THE CHARLESTON BALLET

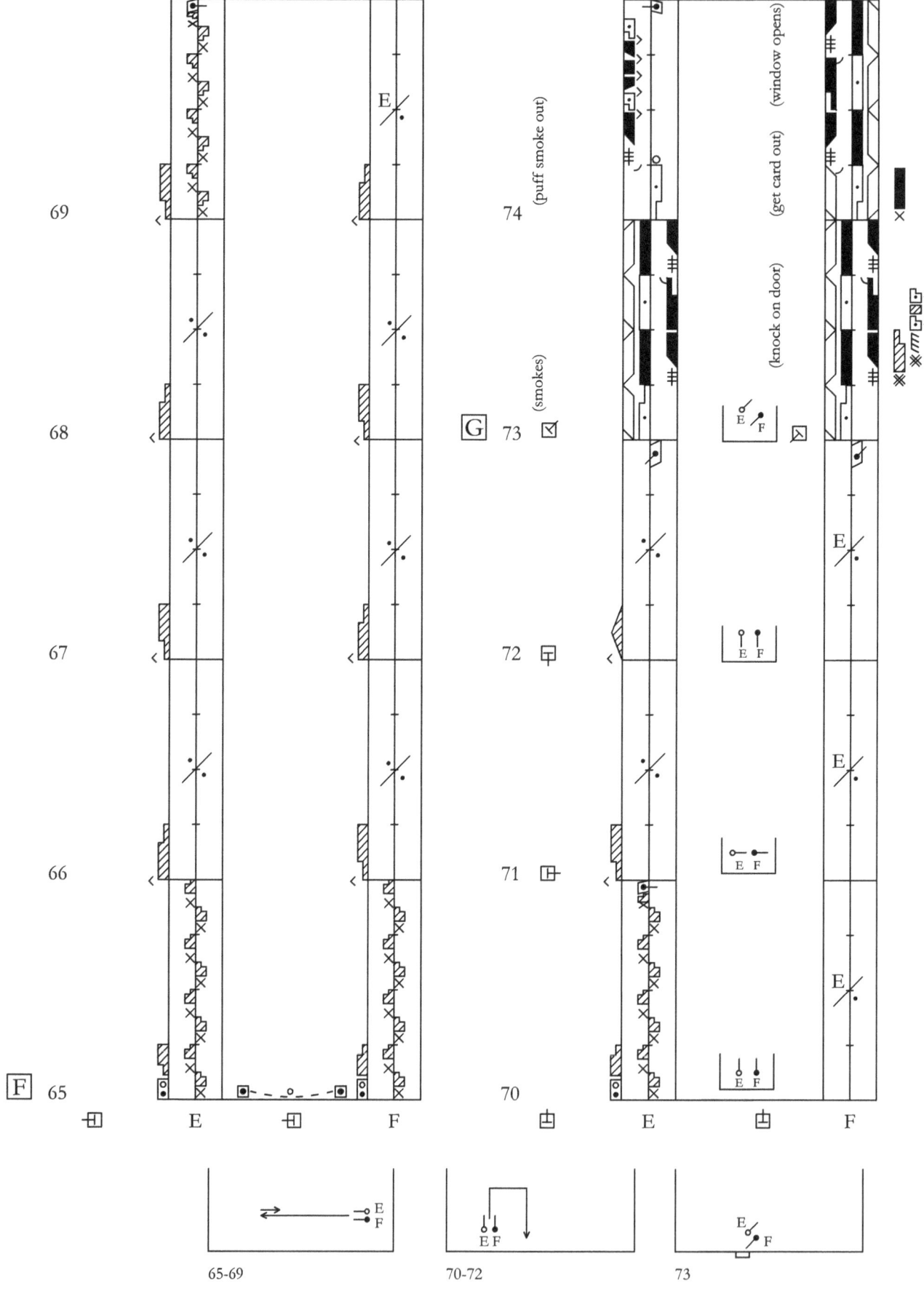

THE DANCE SCORE

29

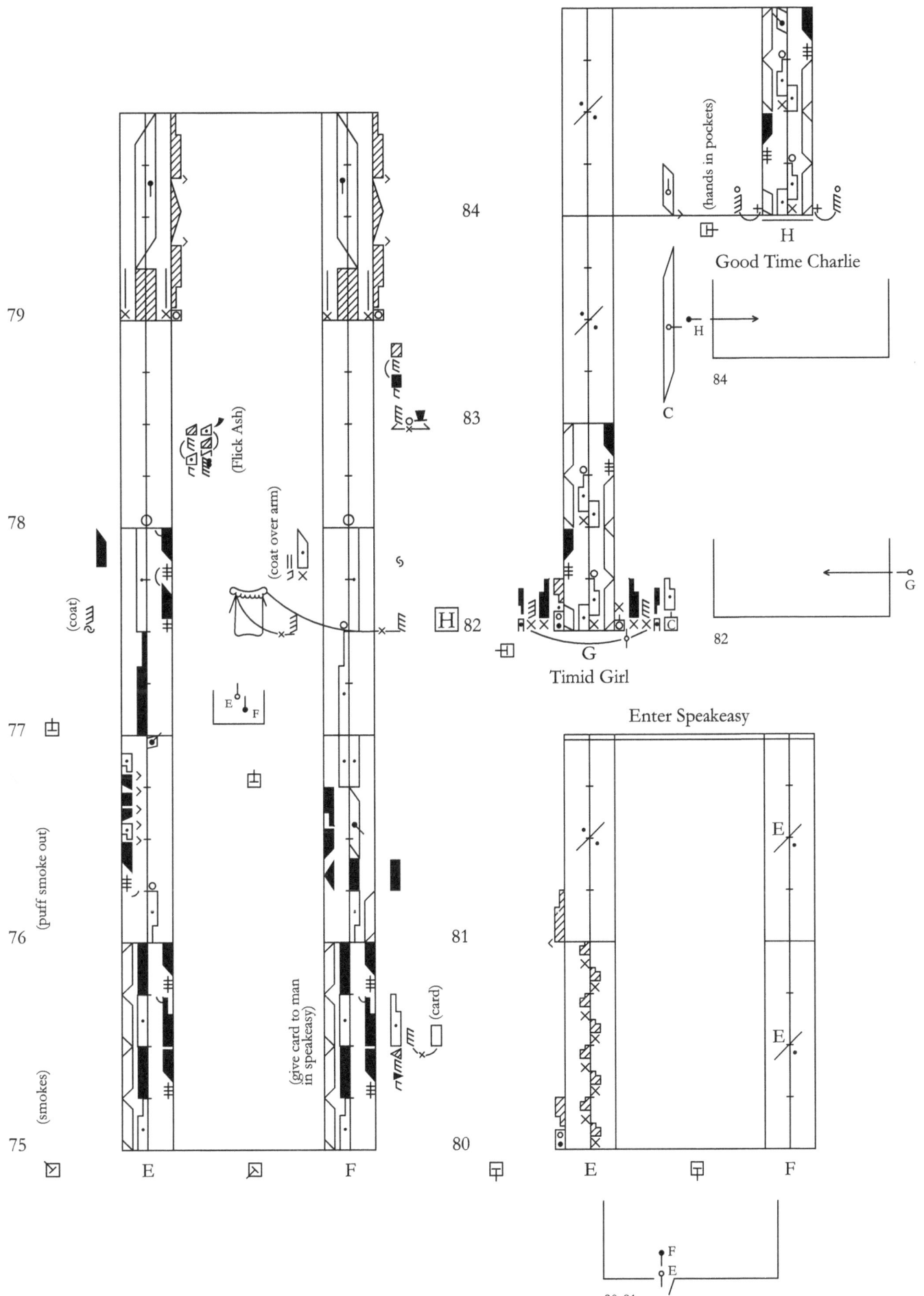

THE CHARLESTON BALLET

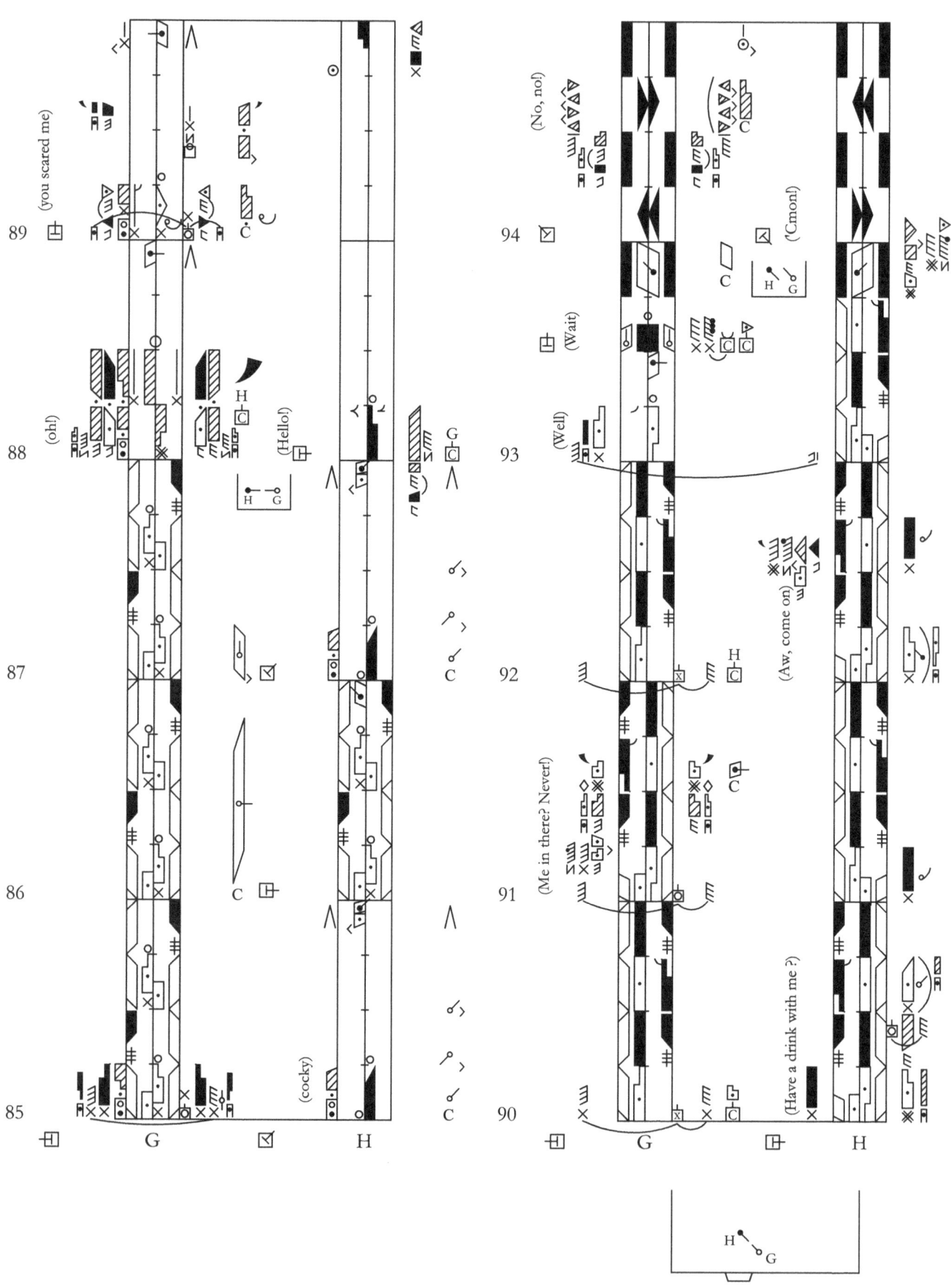

THE DANCE SCORE

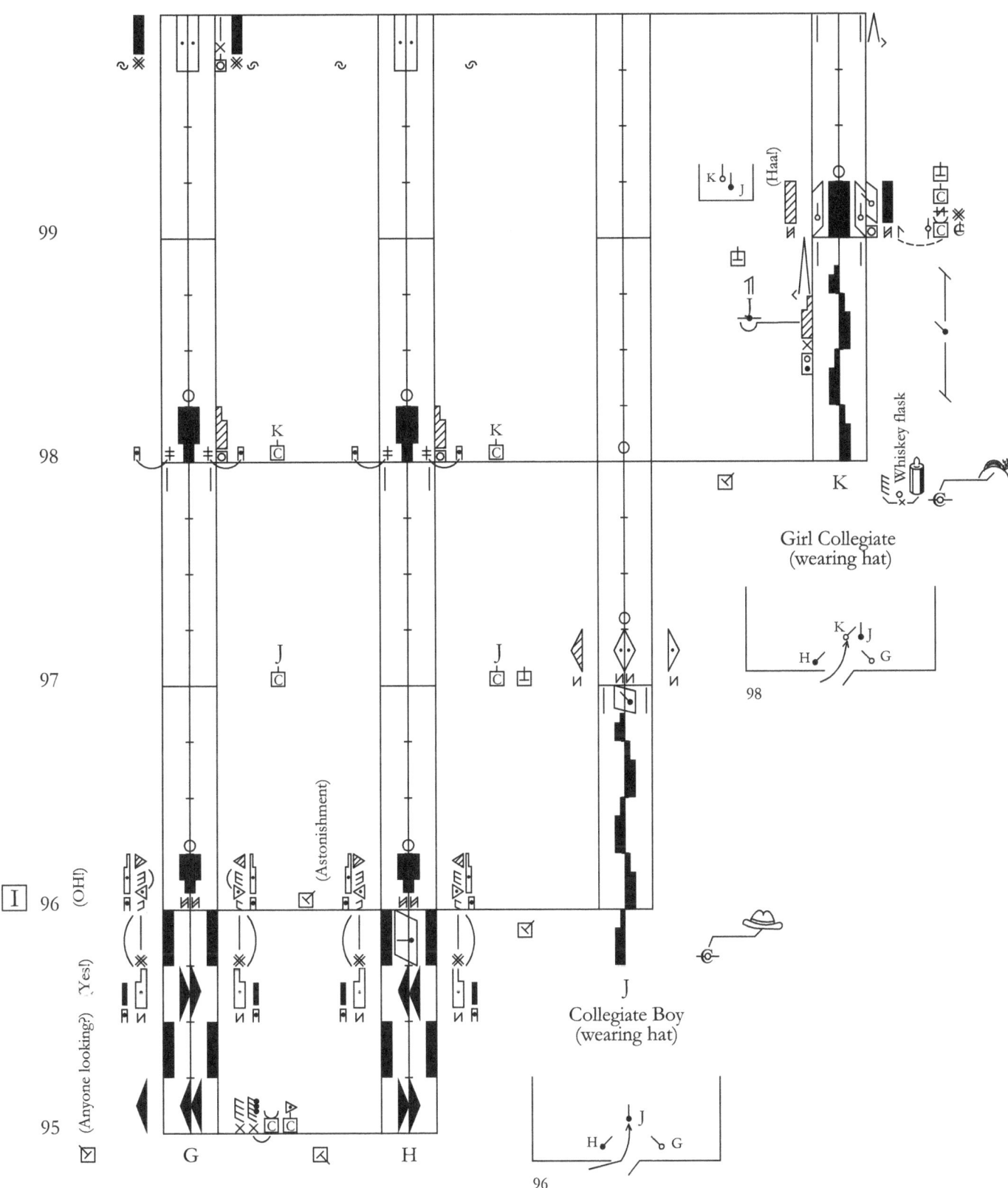

31

THE CHARLESTON BALLET

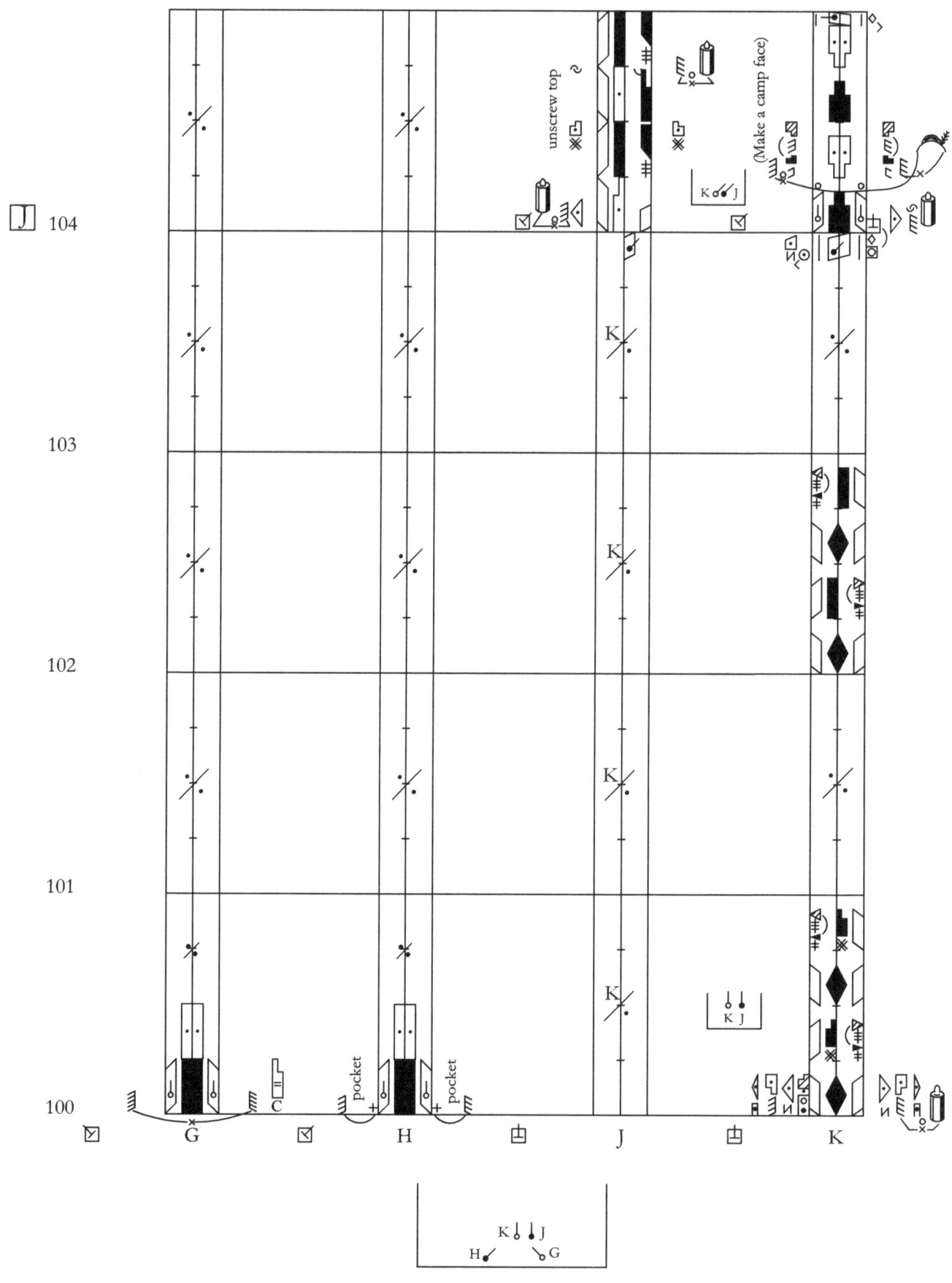

THE DANCE SCORE

33

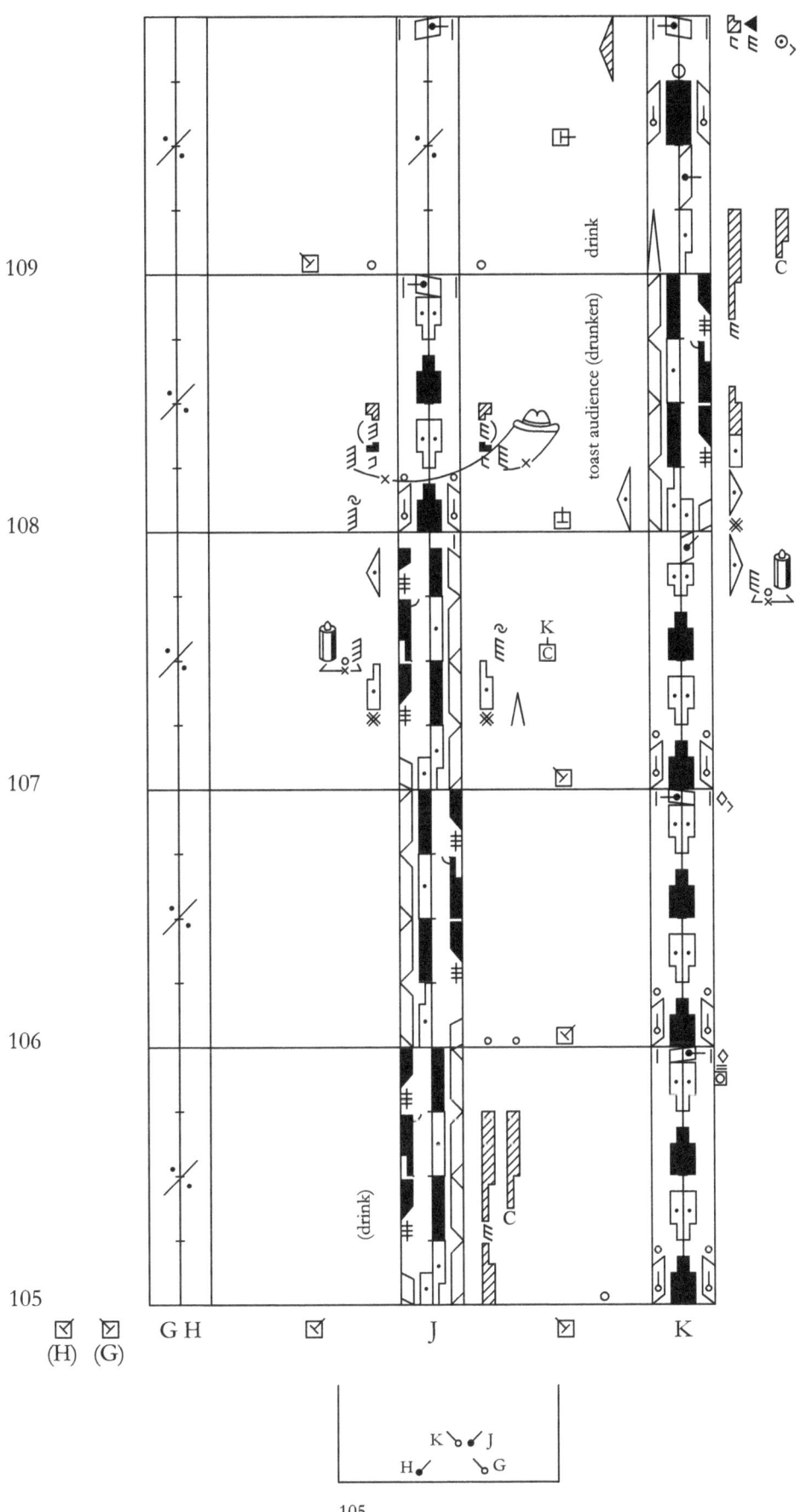

34 THE CHARLESTON BALLET

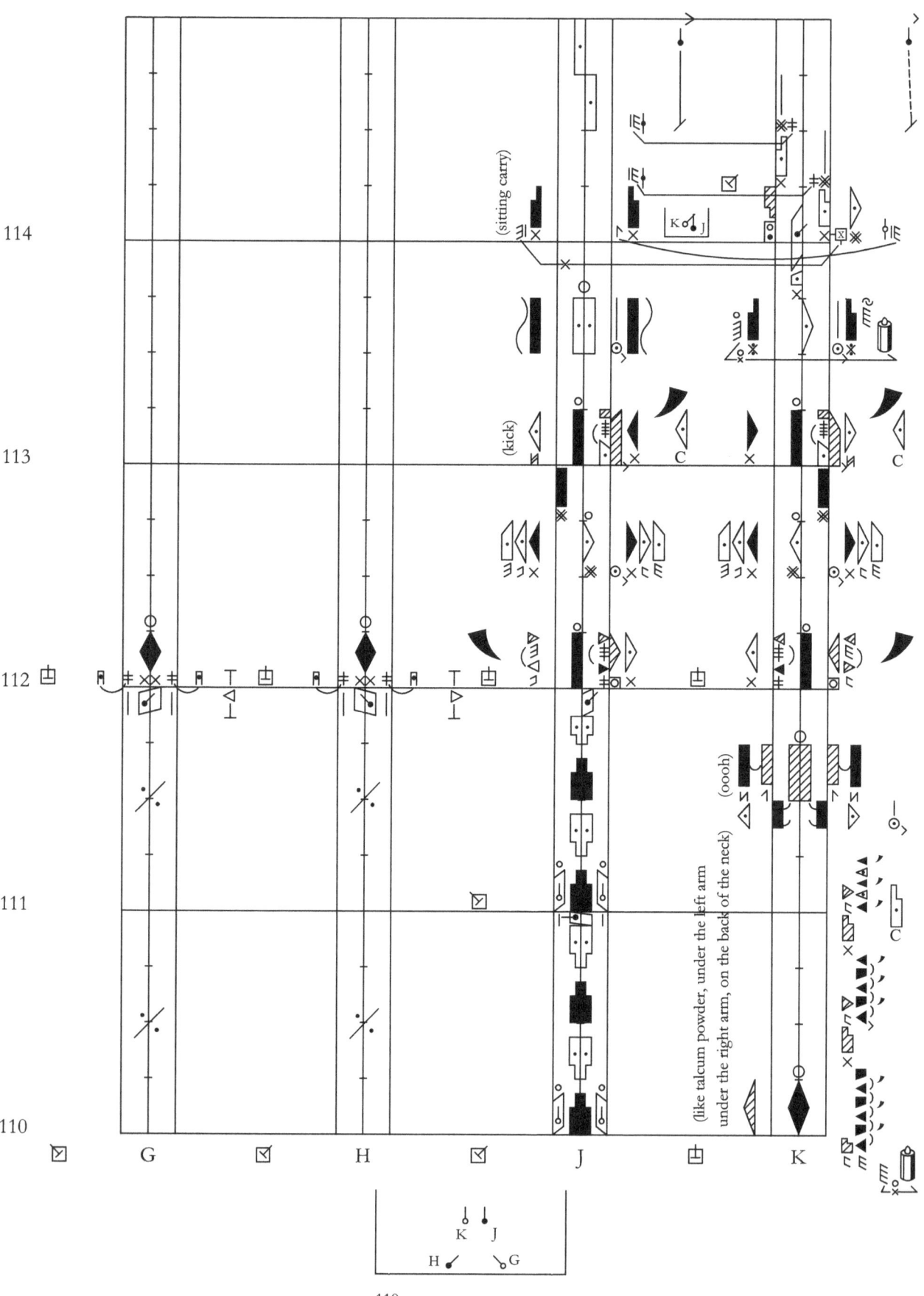

THE DANCE SCORE

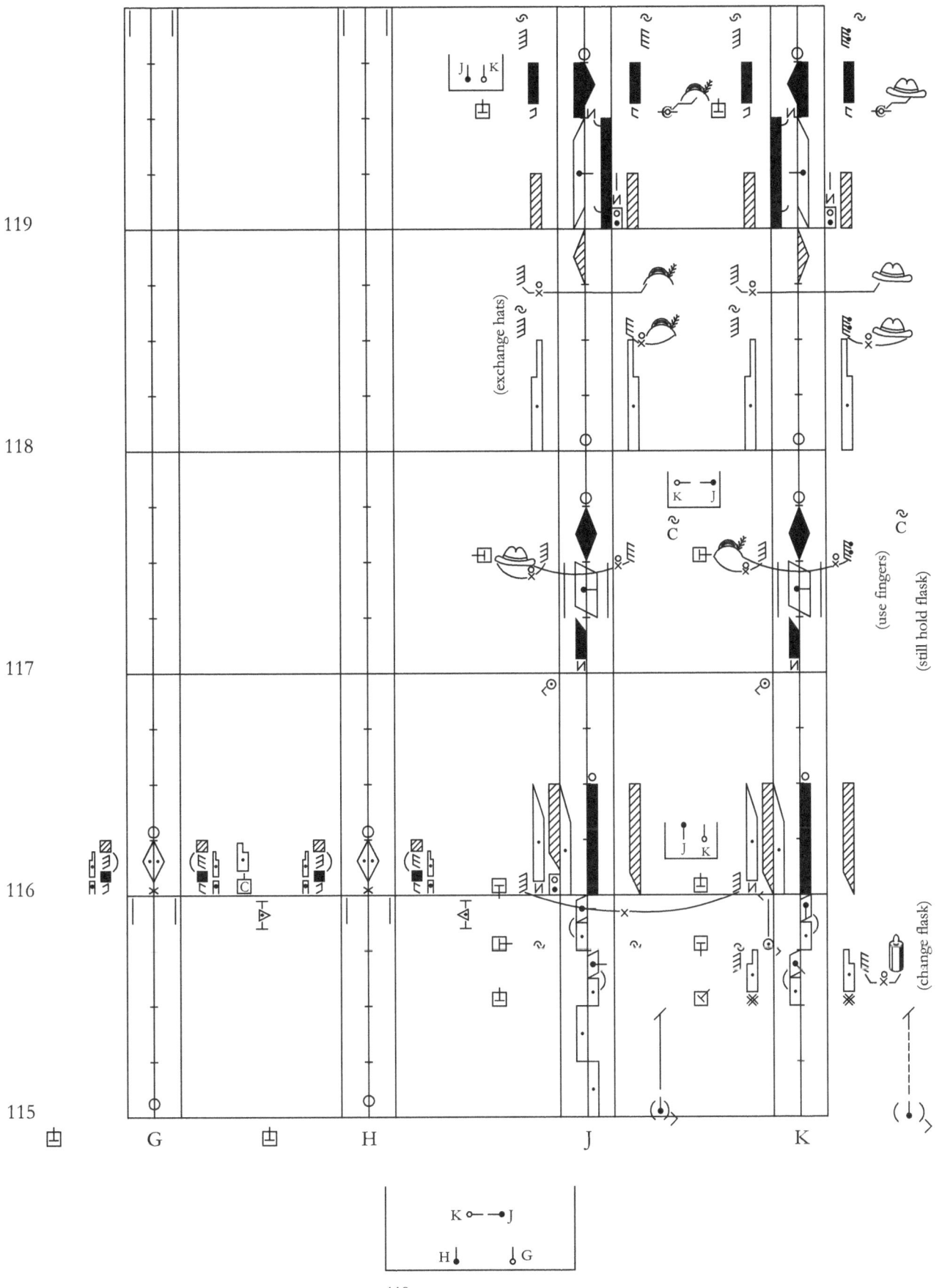

36 THE CHARLESTON BALLET

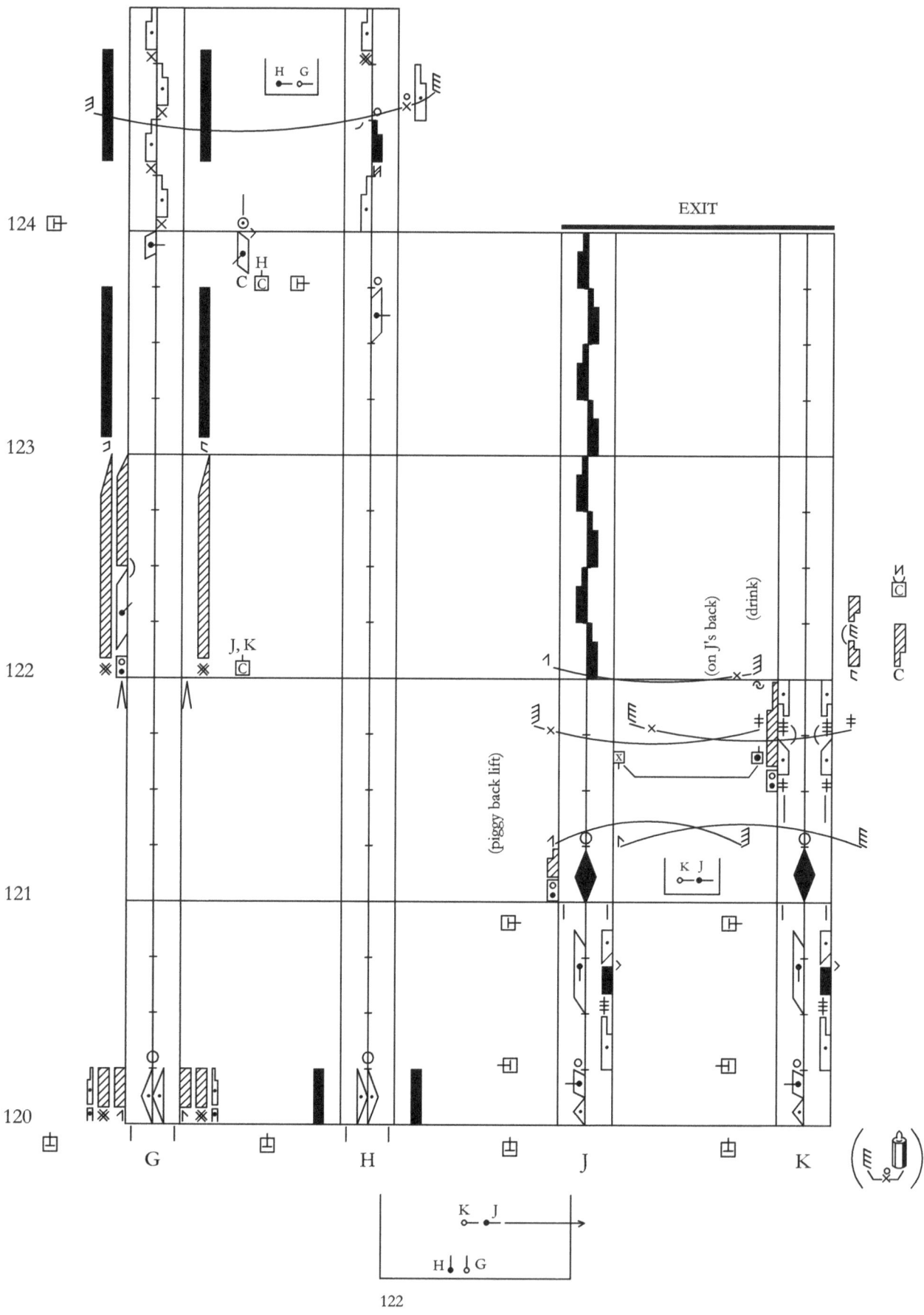

THE DANCE SCORE

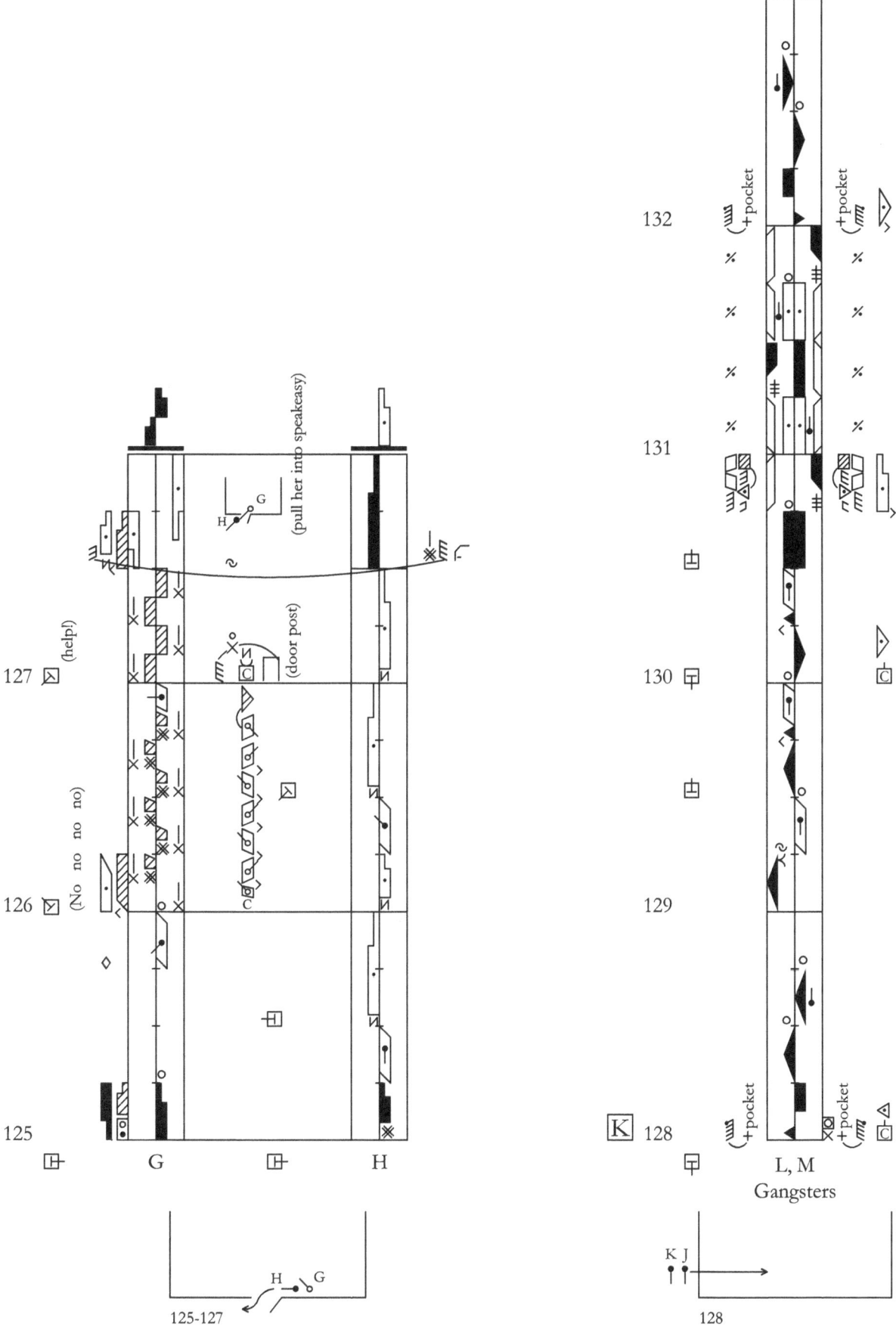

38 THE CHARLESTON BALLET

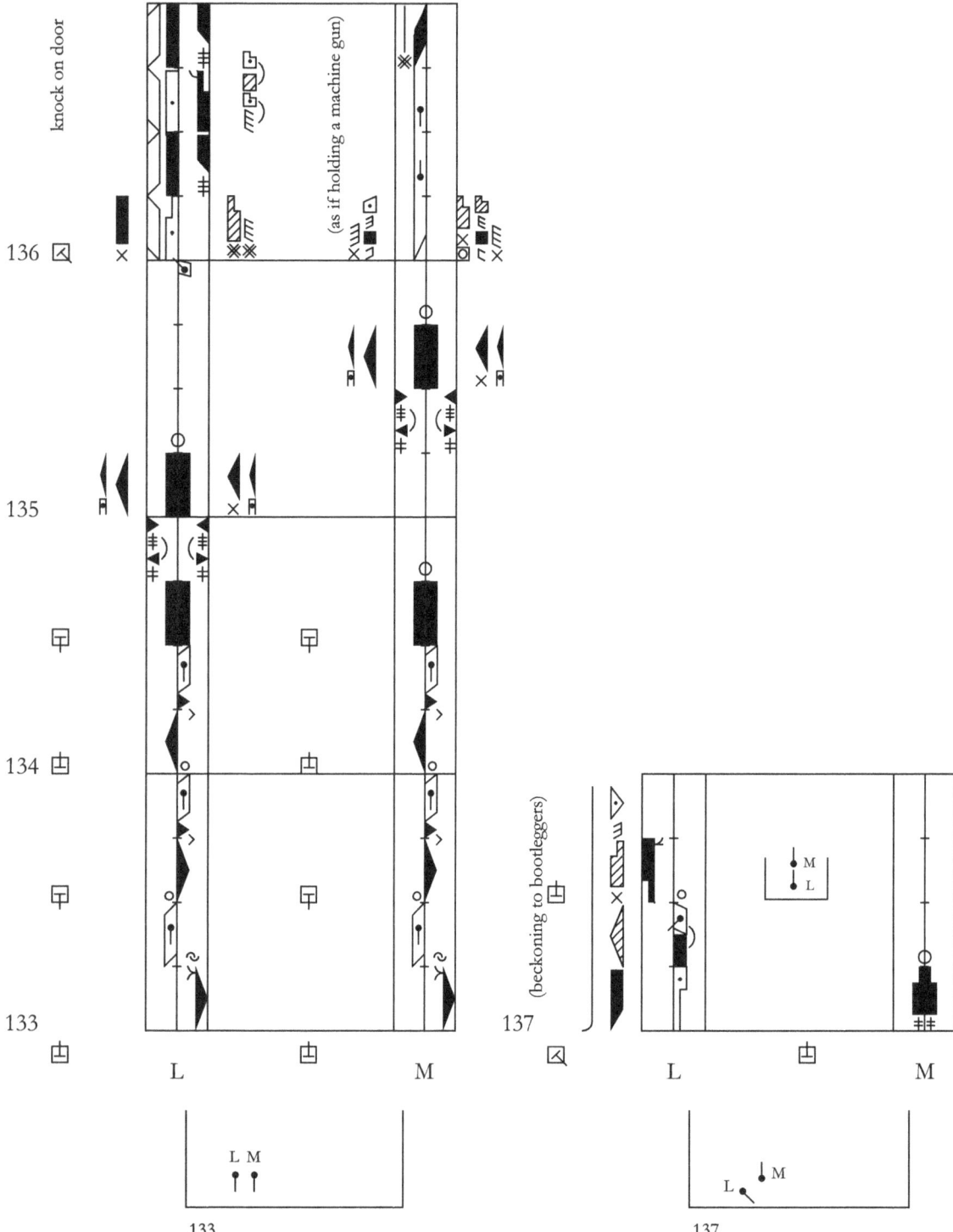

THE DANCE SCORE

39

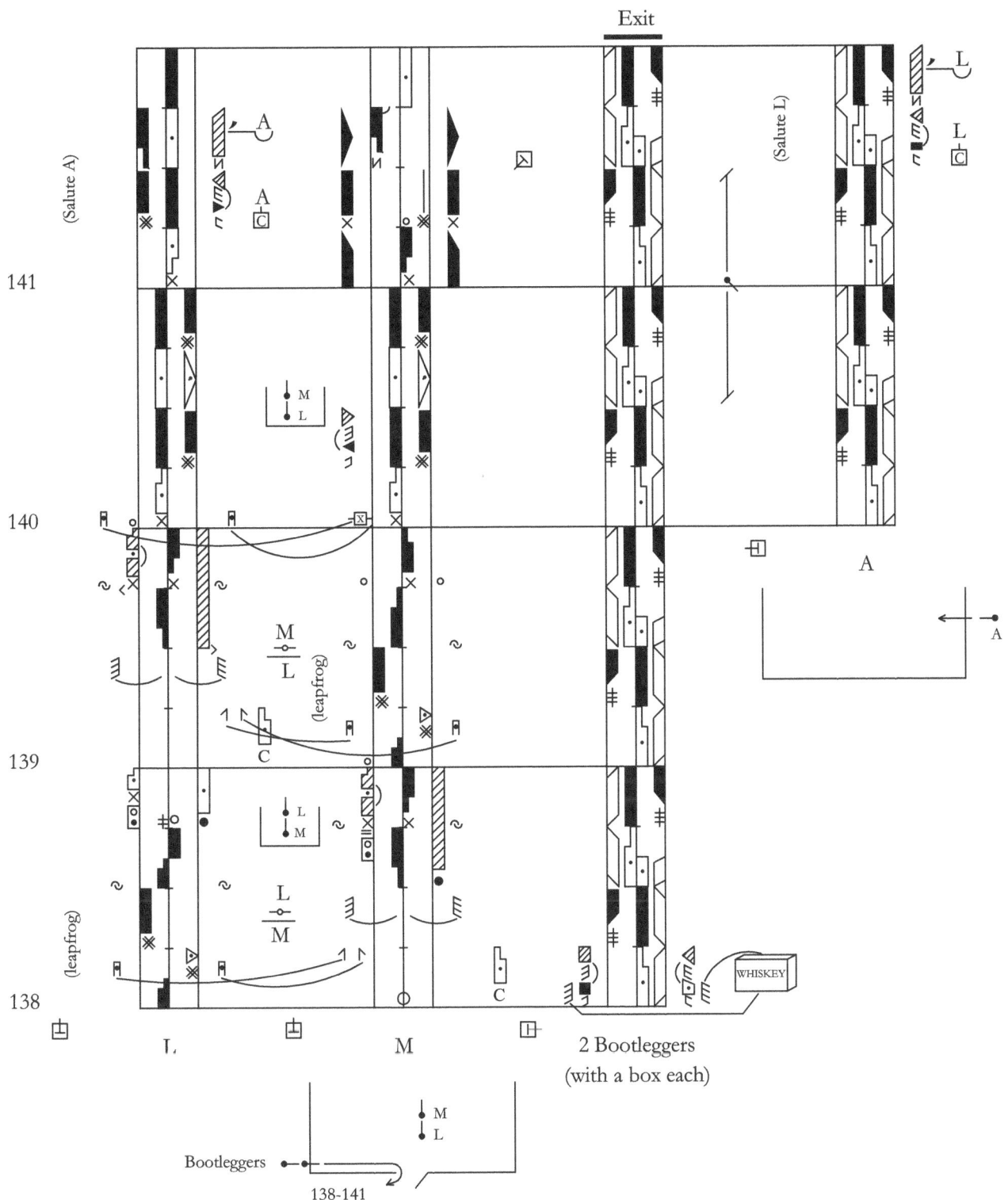

40　　　　　　　THE CHARLESTON BALLET

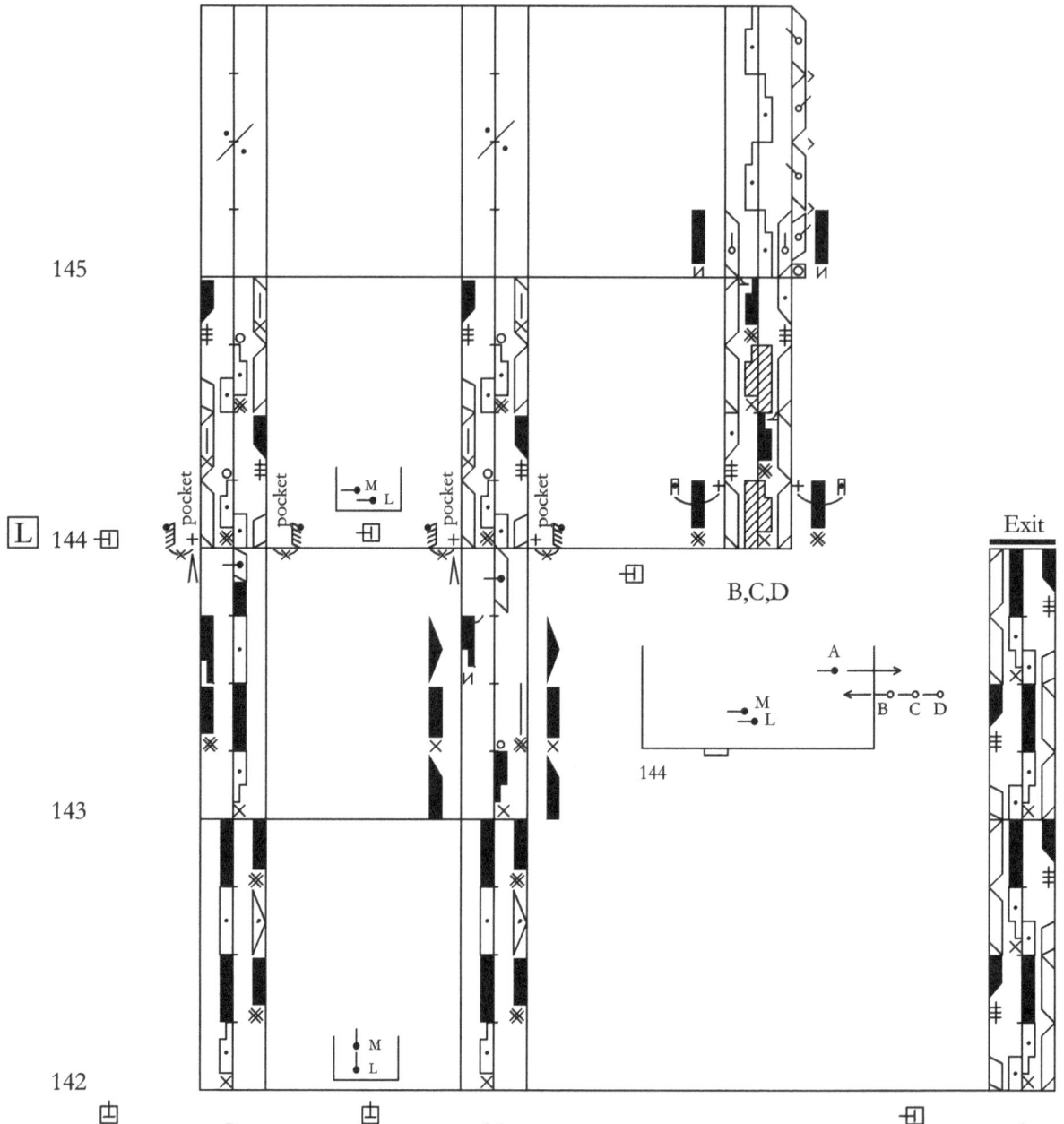

THE DANCE SCORE

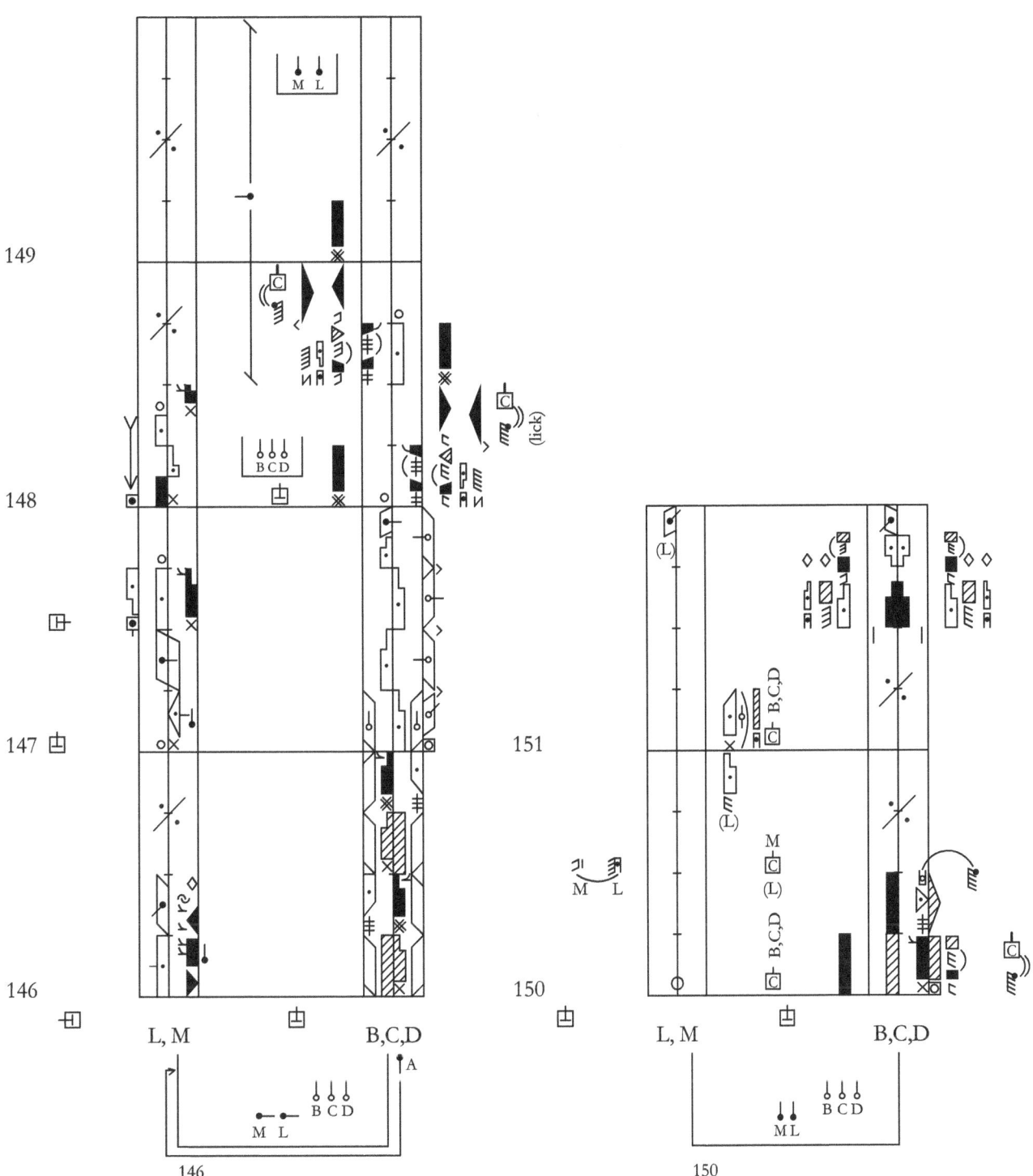

THE CHARLESTON BALLET

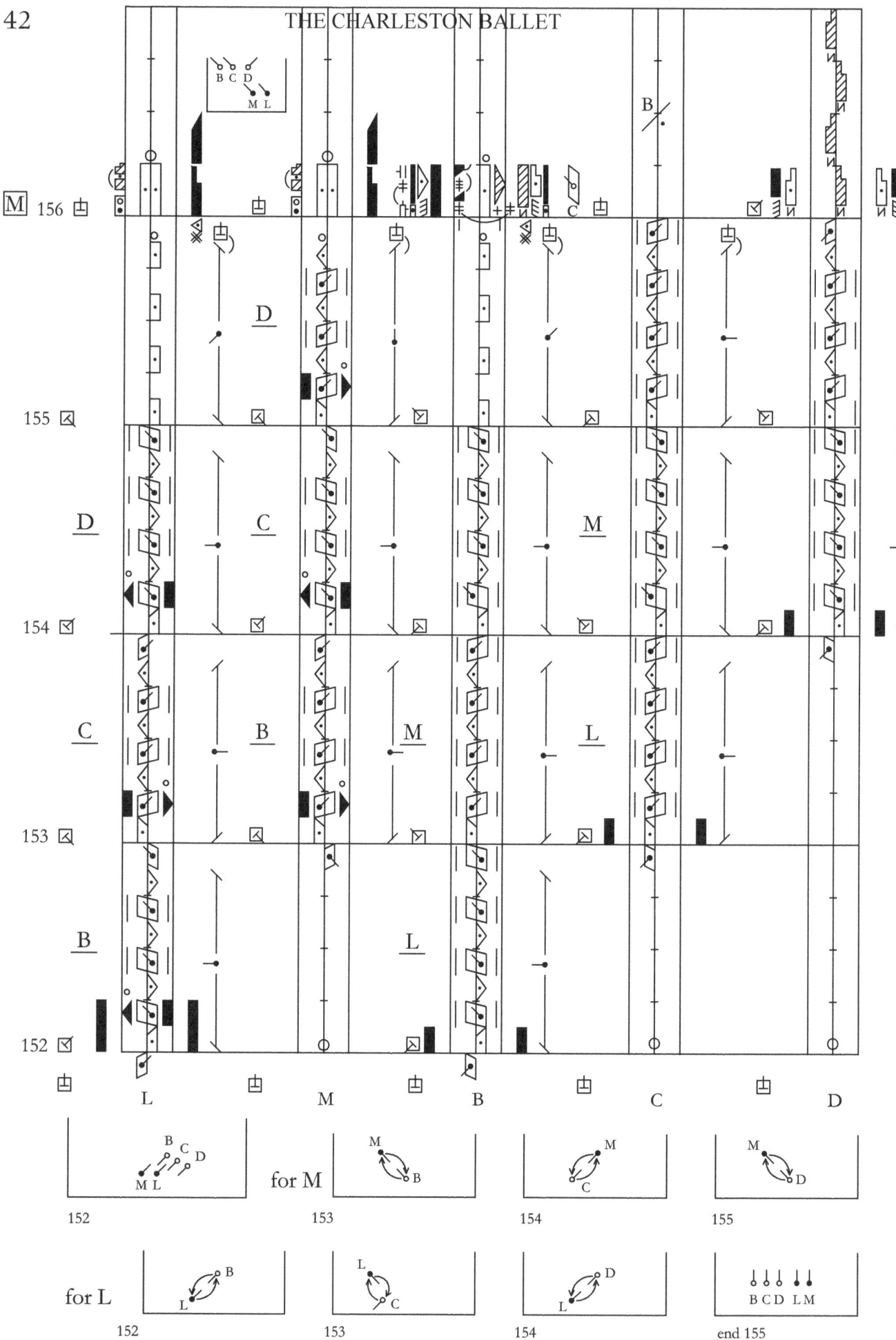

THE DANCE SCORE

43

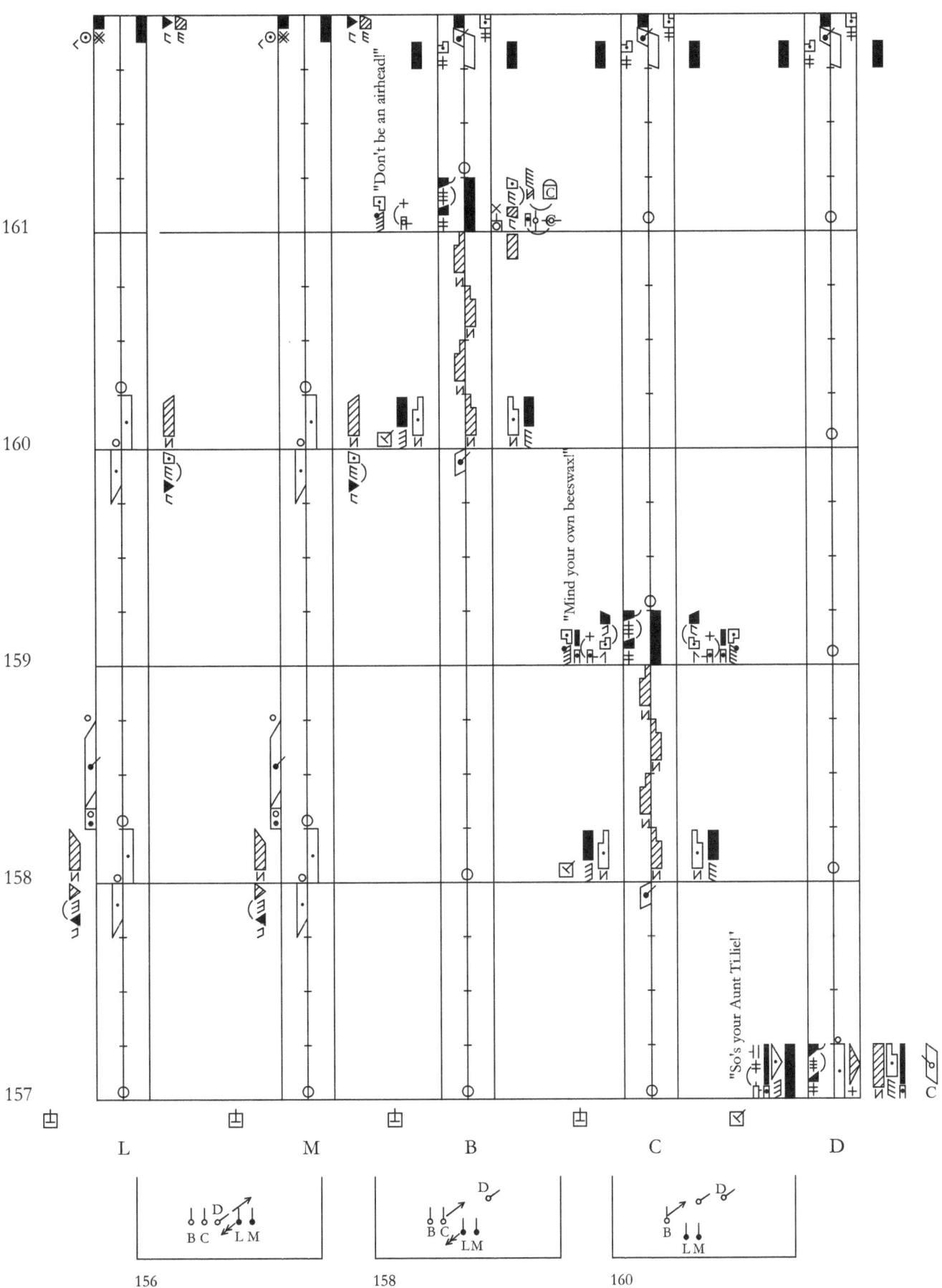

44 THE CHARLESTON BALLET

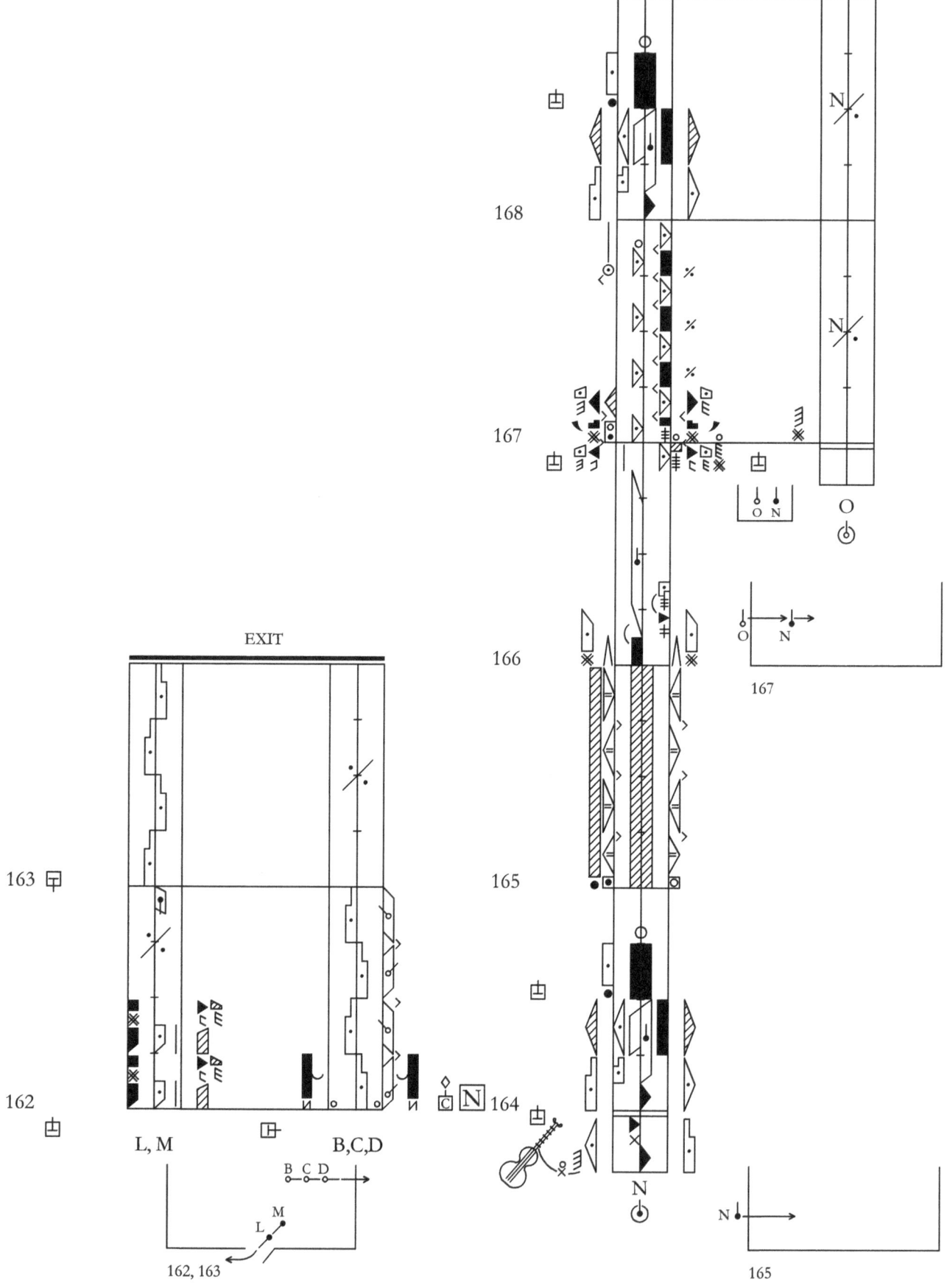

THE DANCE SCORE

45

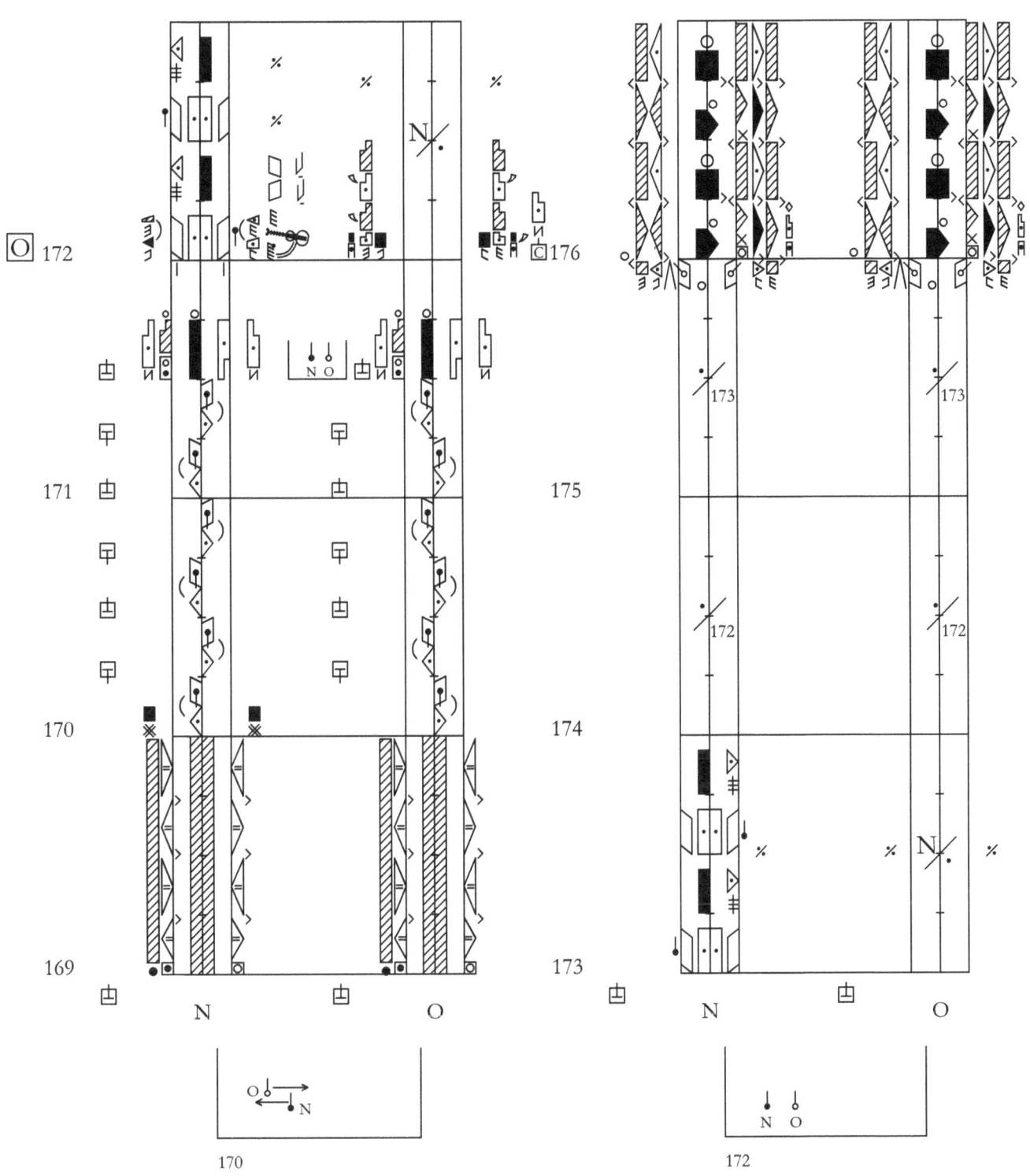

46 THE CHARLESTON BALLET

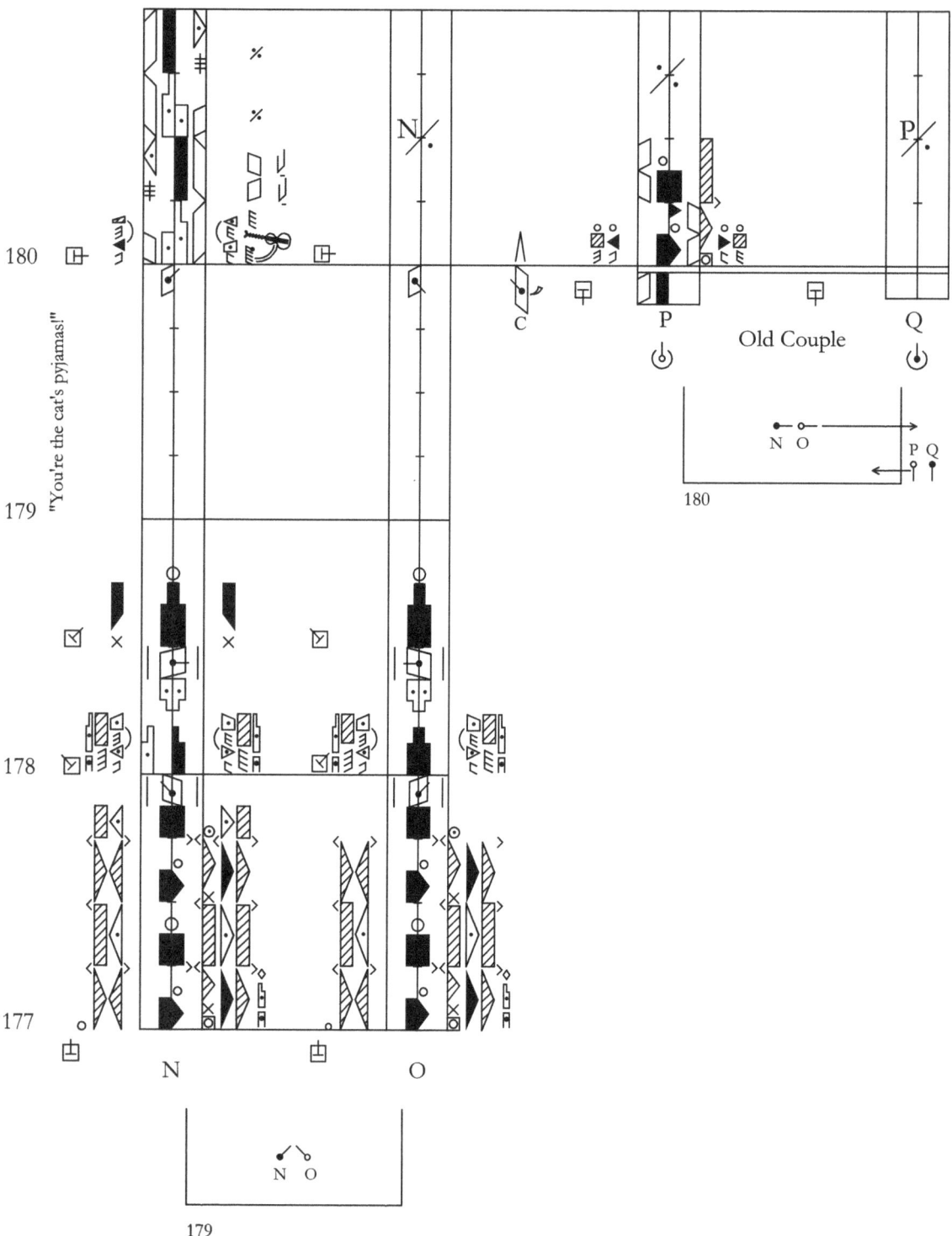

THE DANCE SCORE 47

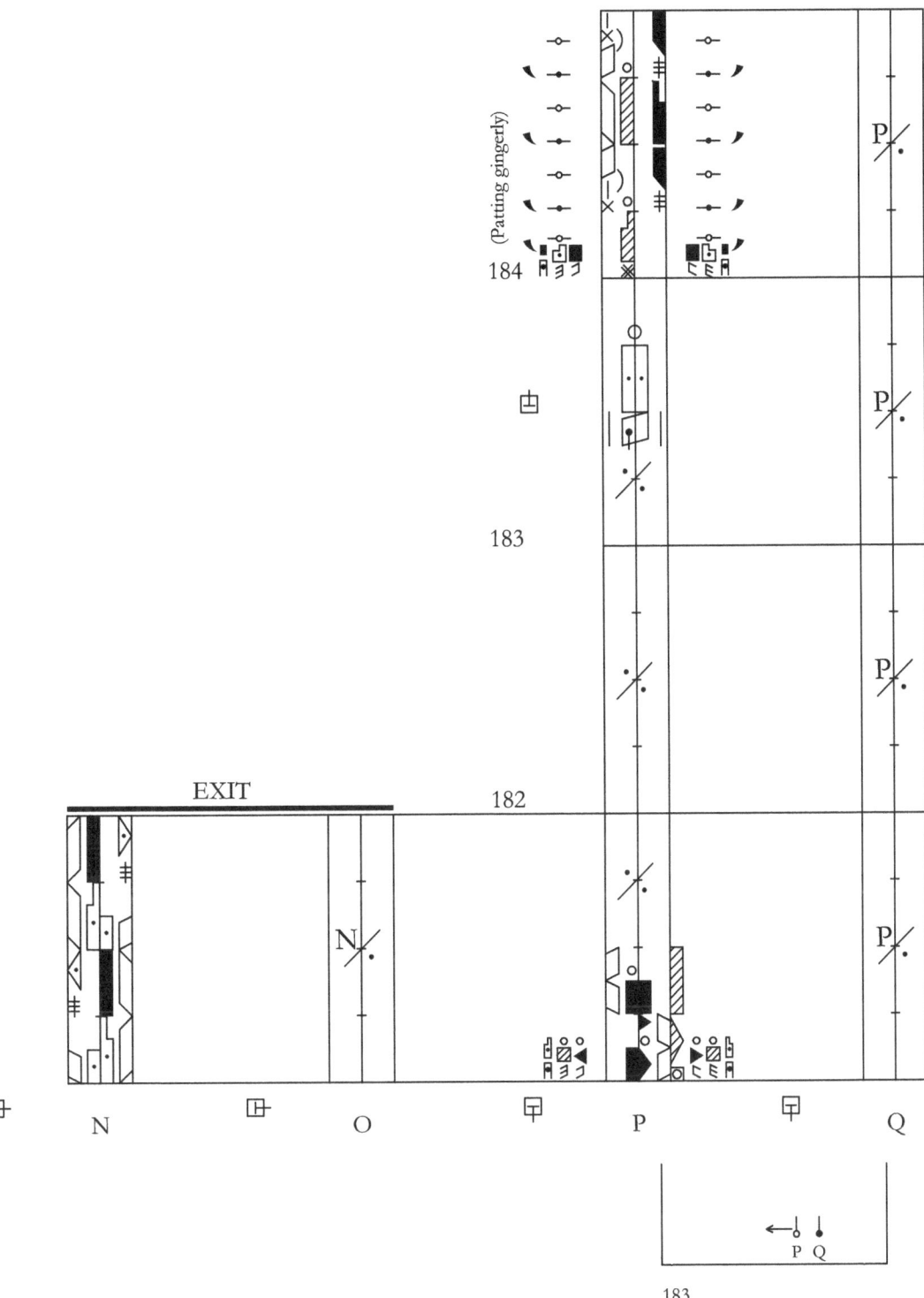

48 THE CHARLESTON BALLET

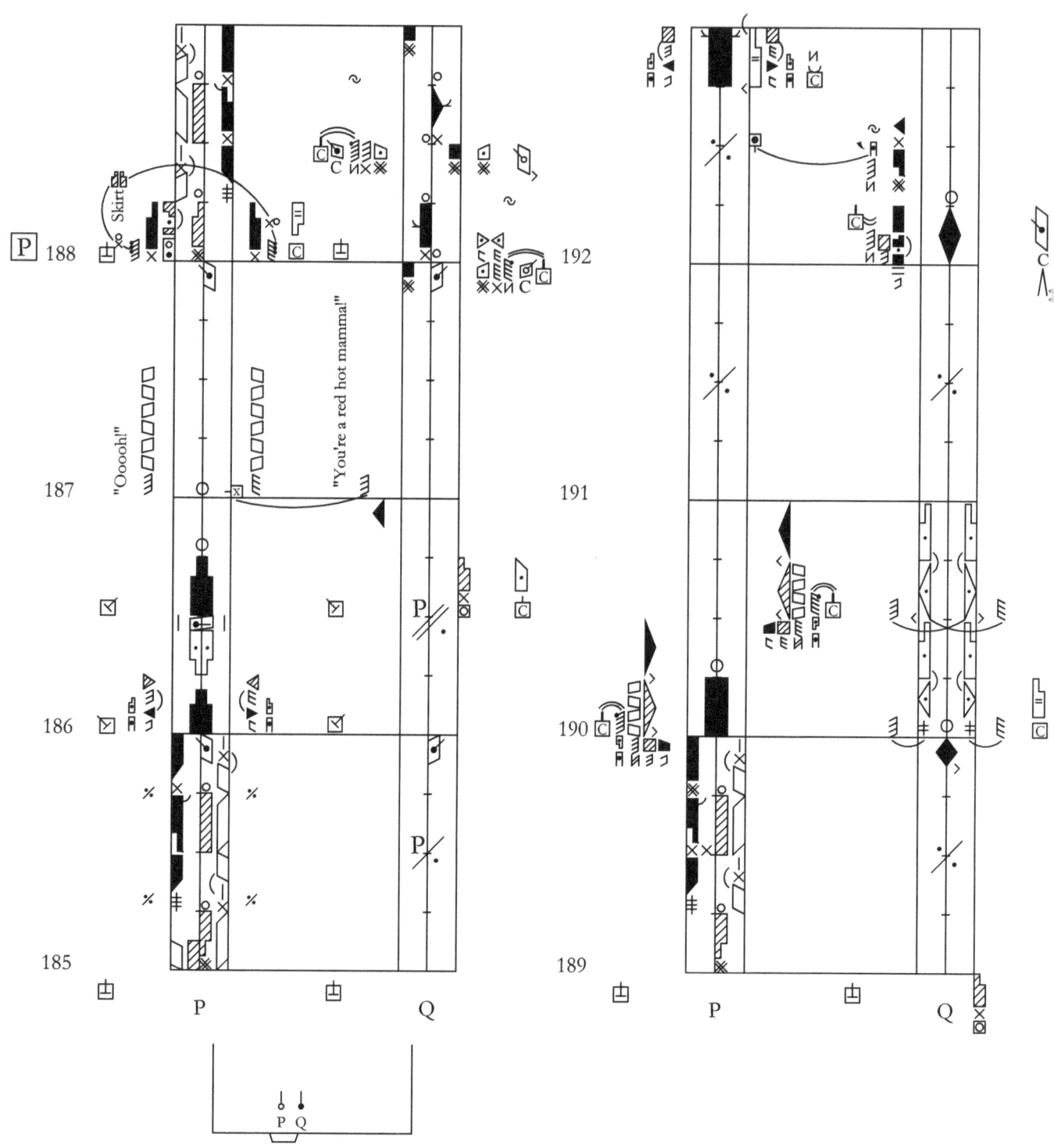

THE DANCE SCORE

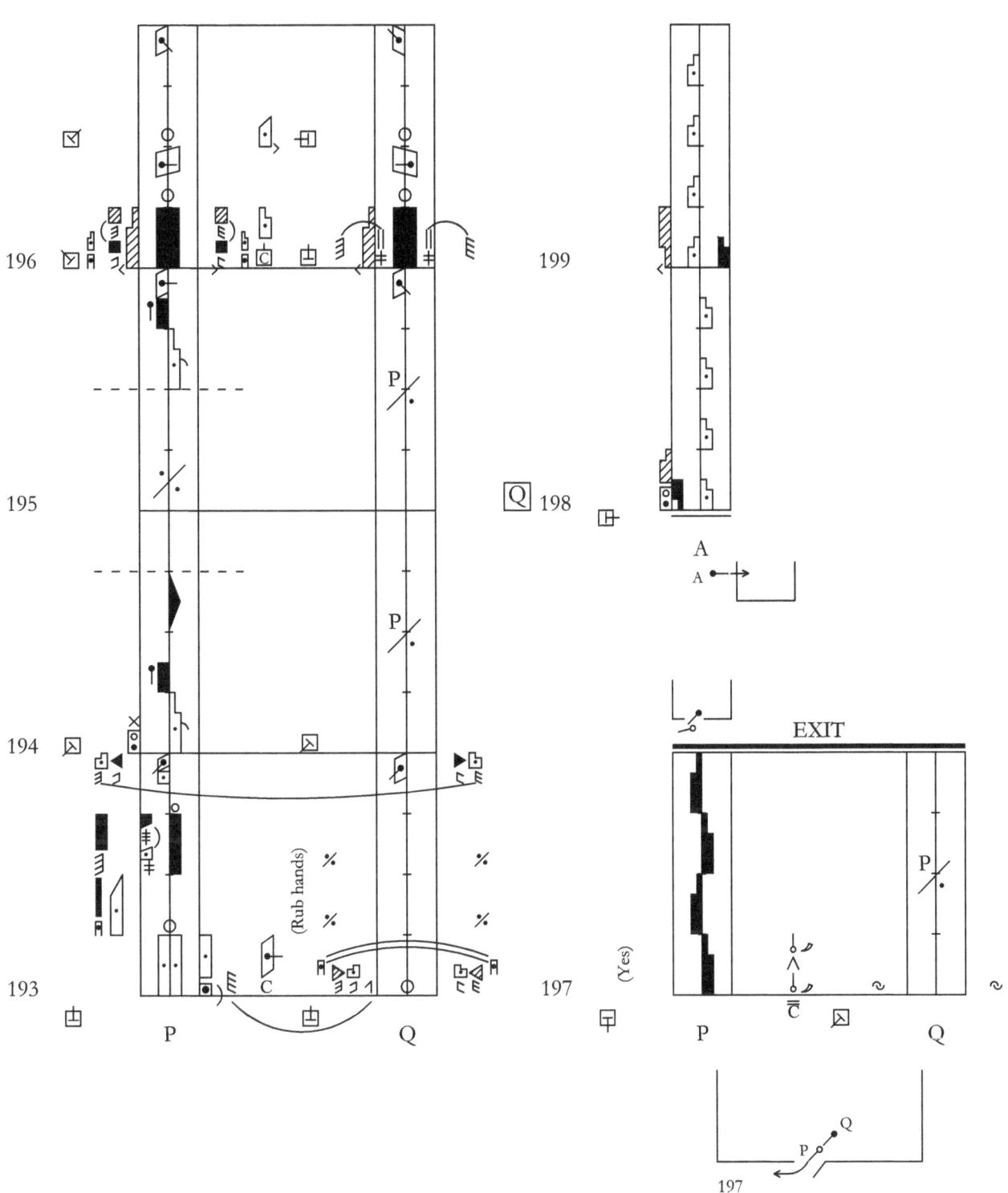

50 THE CHARLESTON BALLET

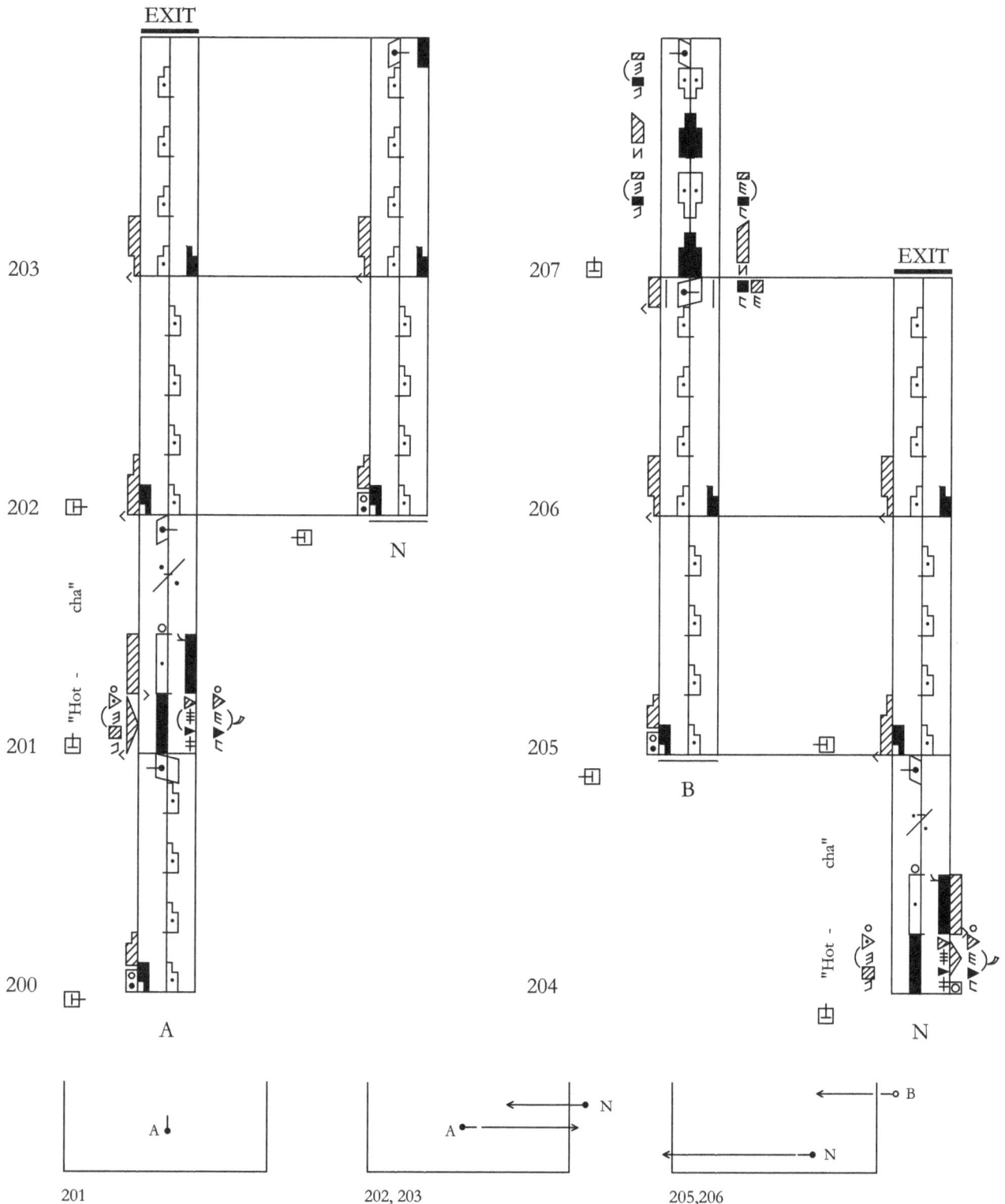

THE DANCE SCORE

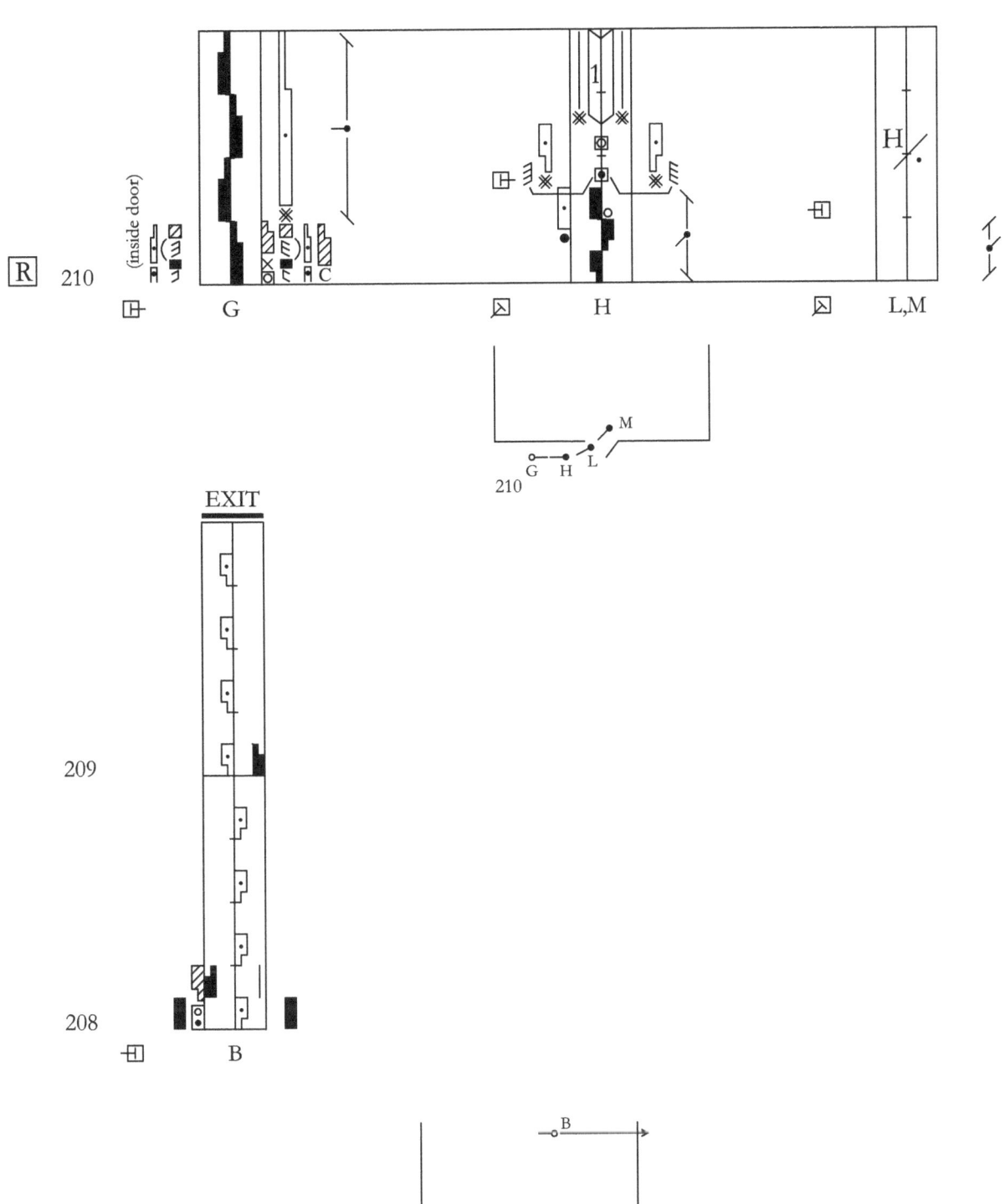

52 THE CHARLESTON BALLET

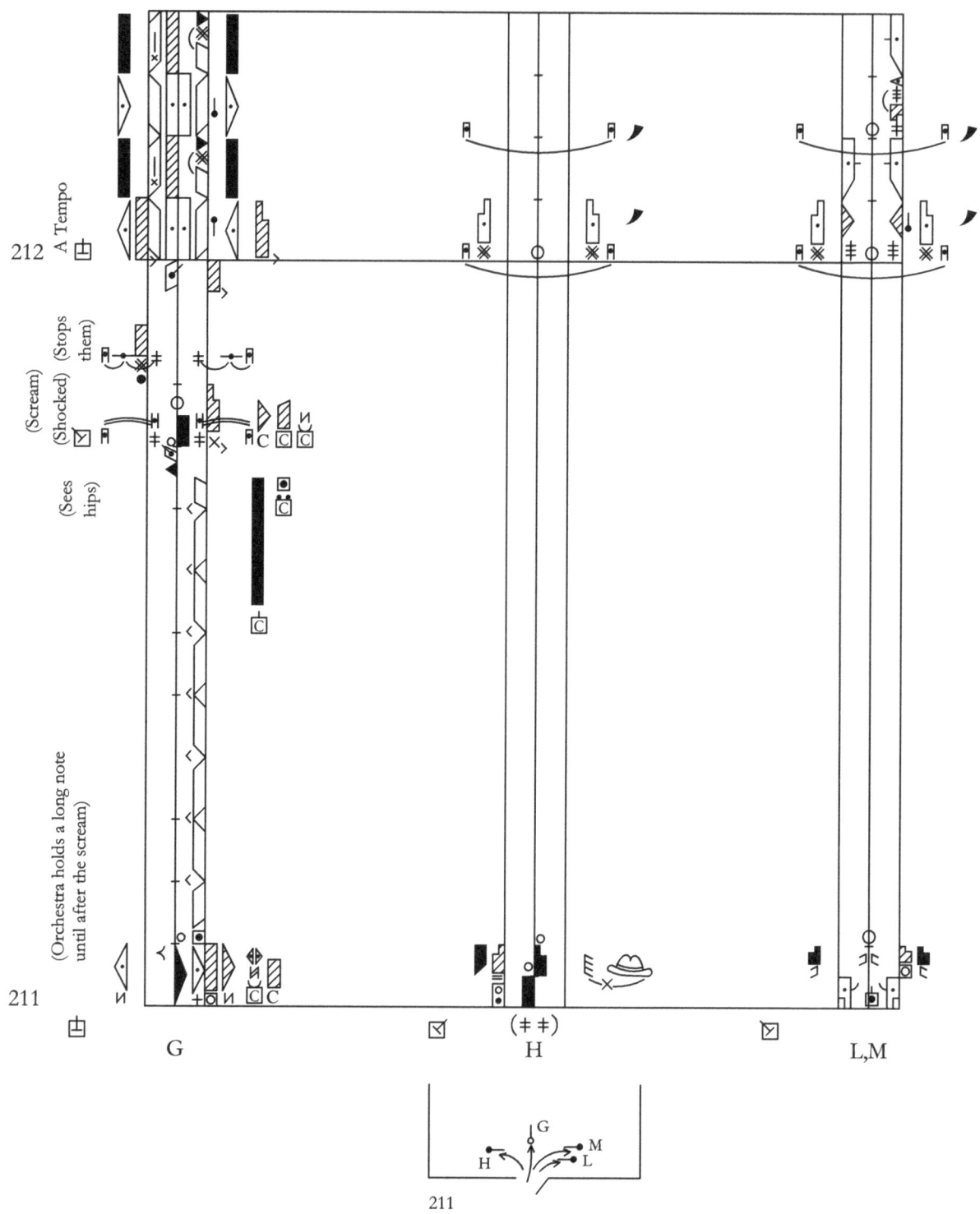

THE DANCE SCORE

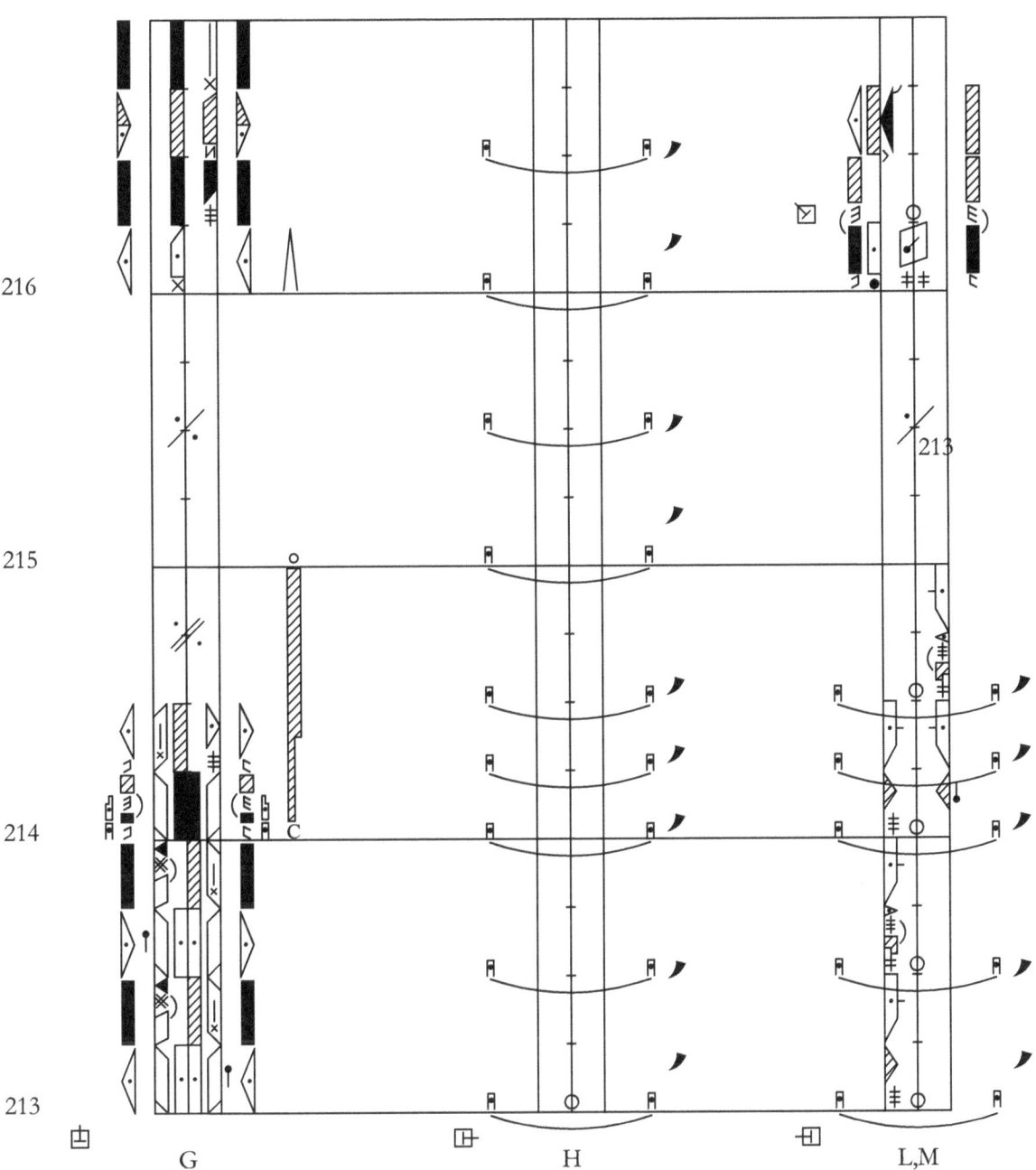

54 THE CHARLESTON BALLET

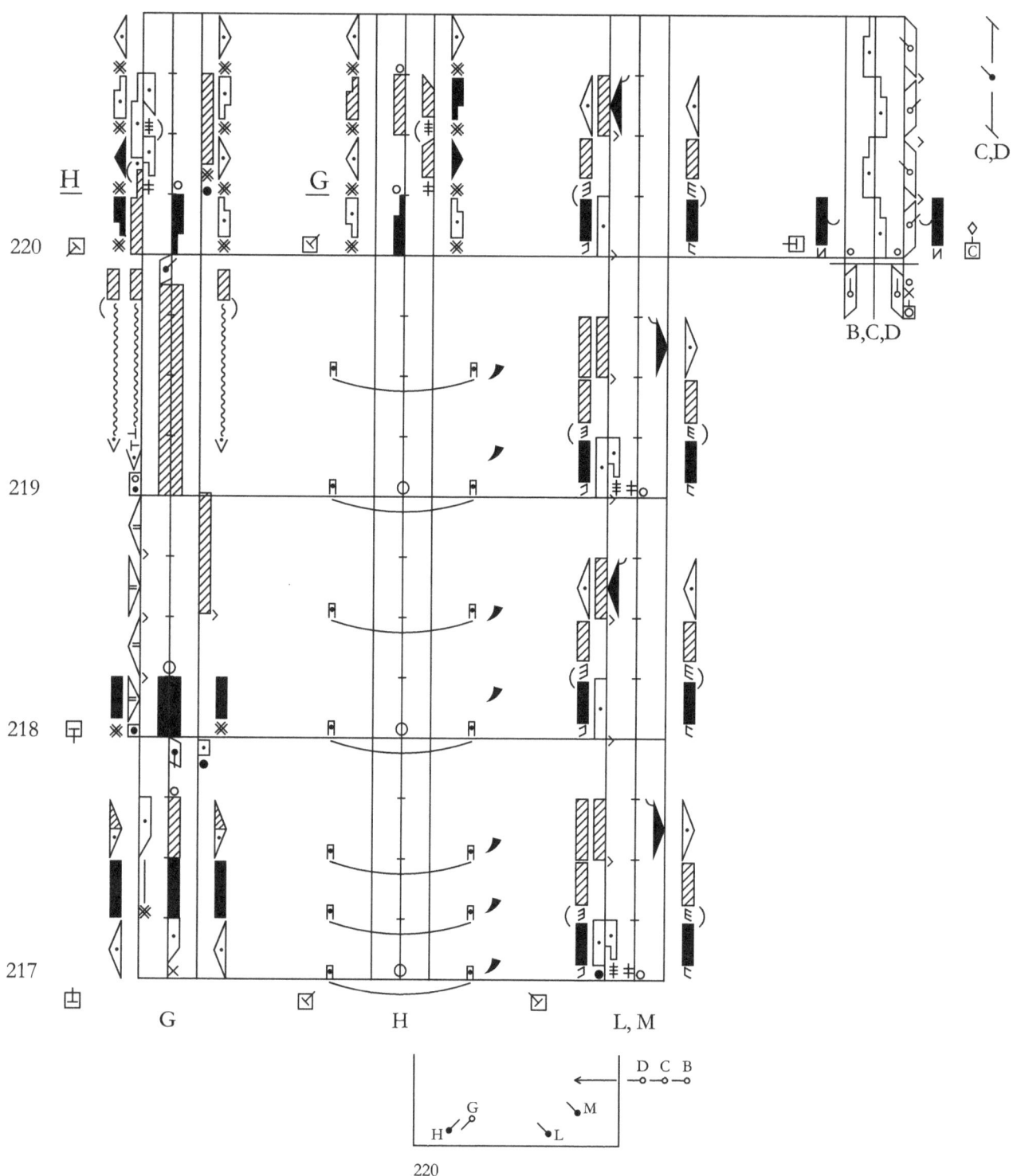

THE DANCE SCORE 55

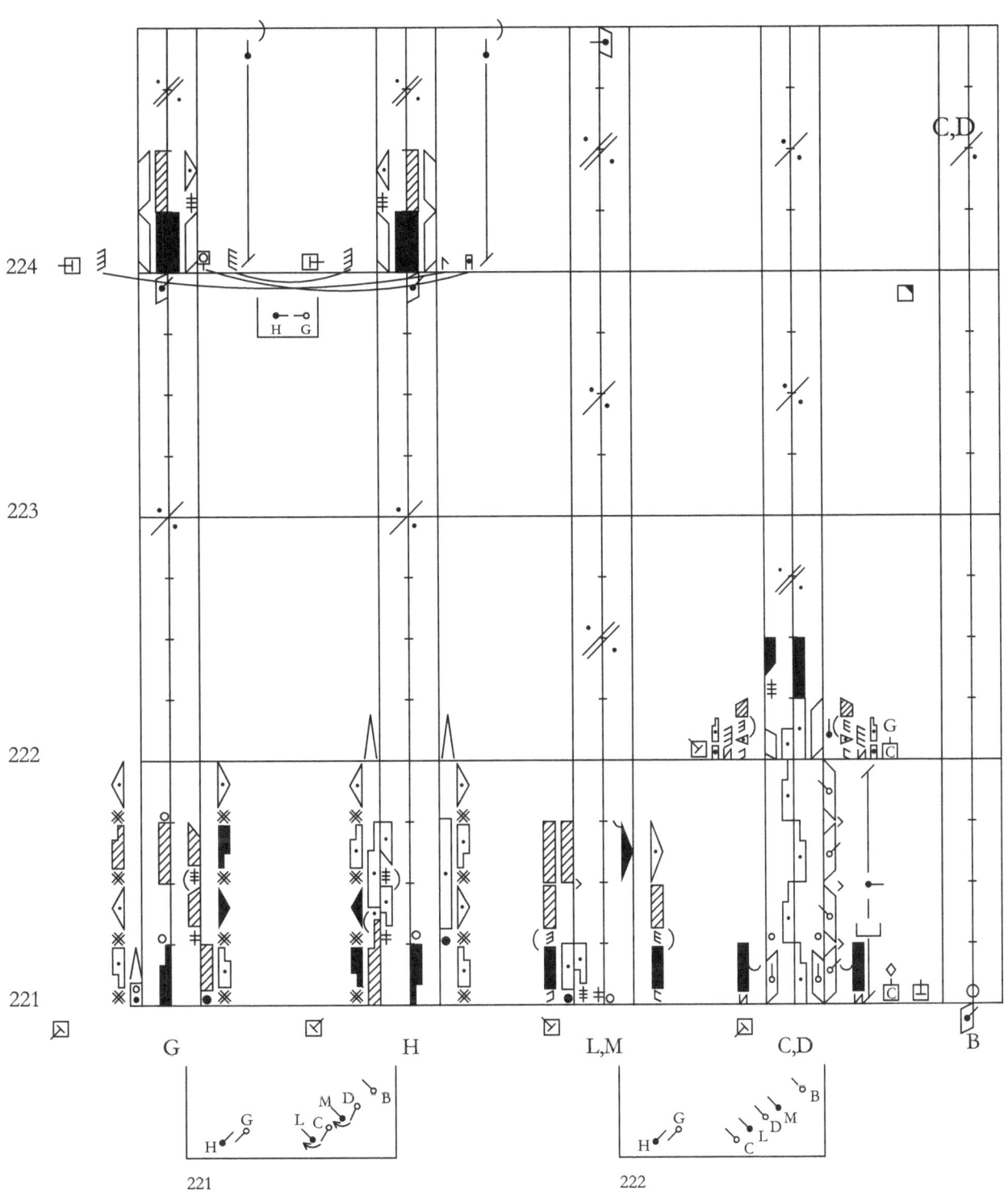

56 THE CHARLESTON BALLET

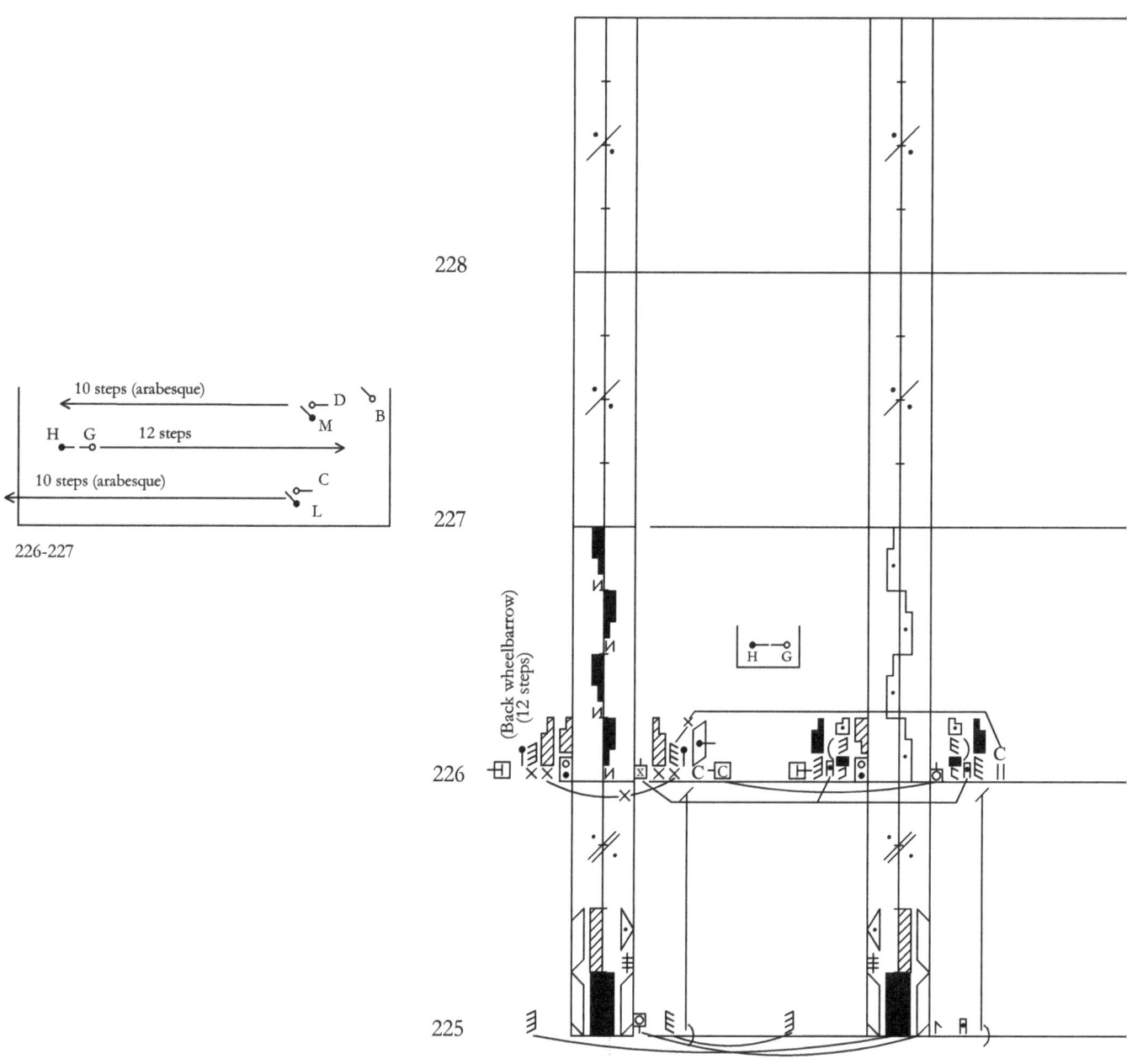

THE DANCE SCORE

57

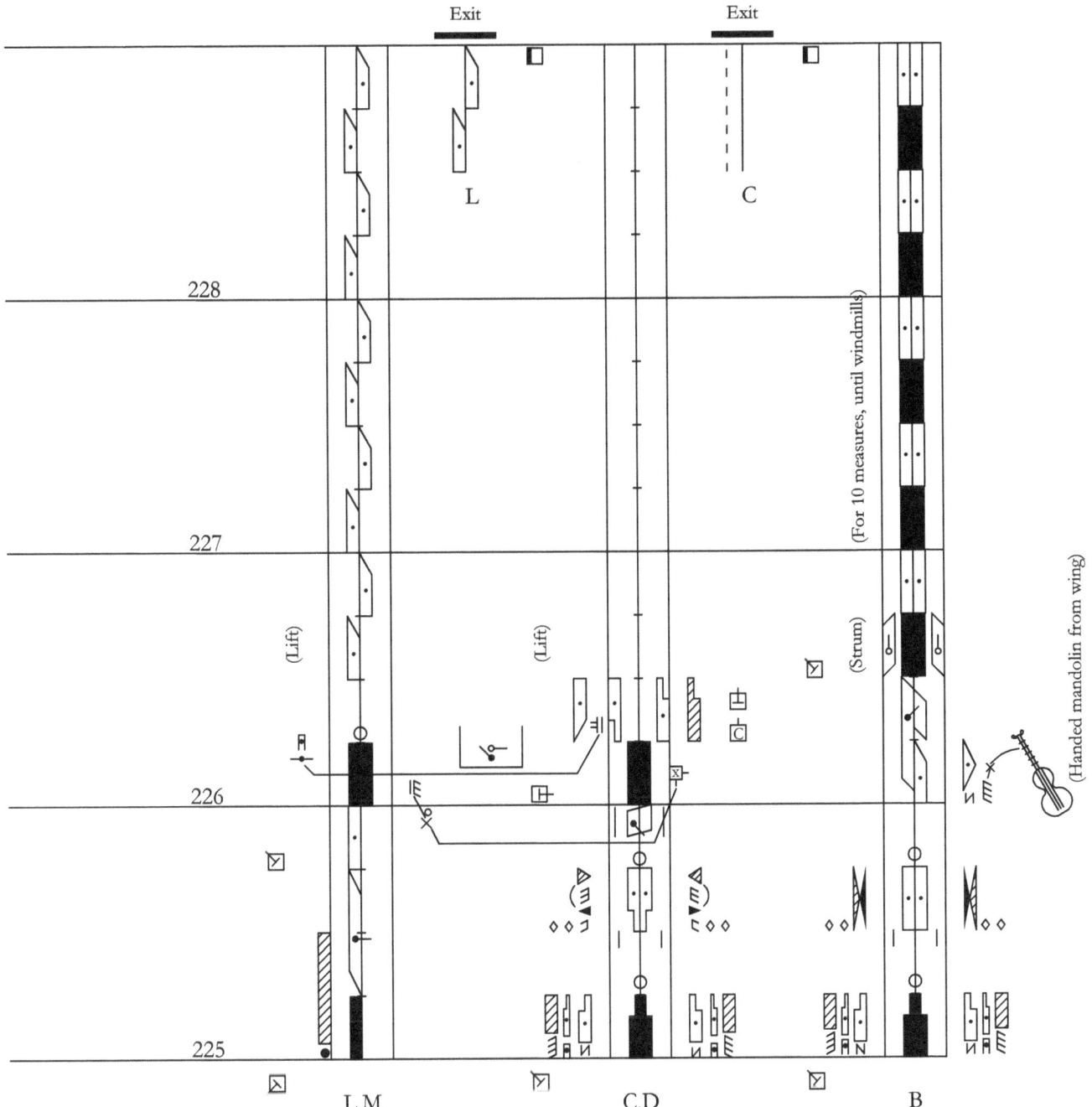

58 THE CHARLESTON BALLET

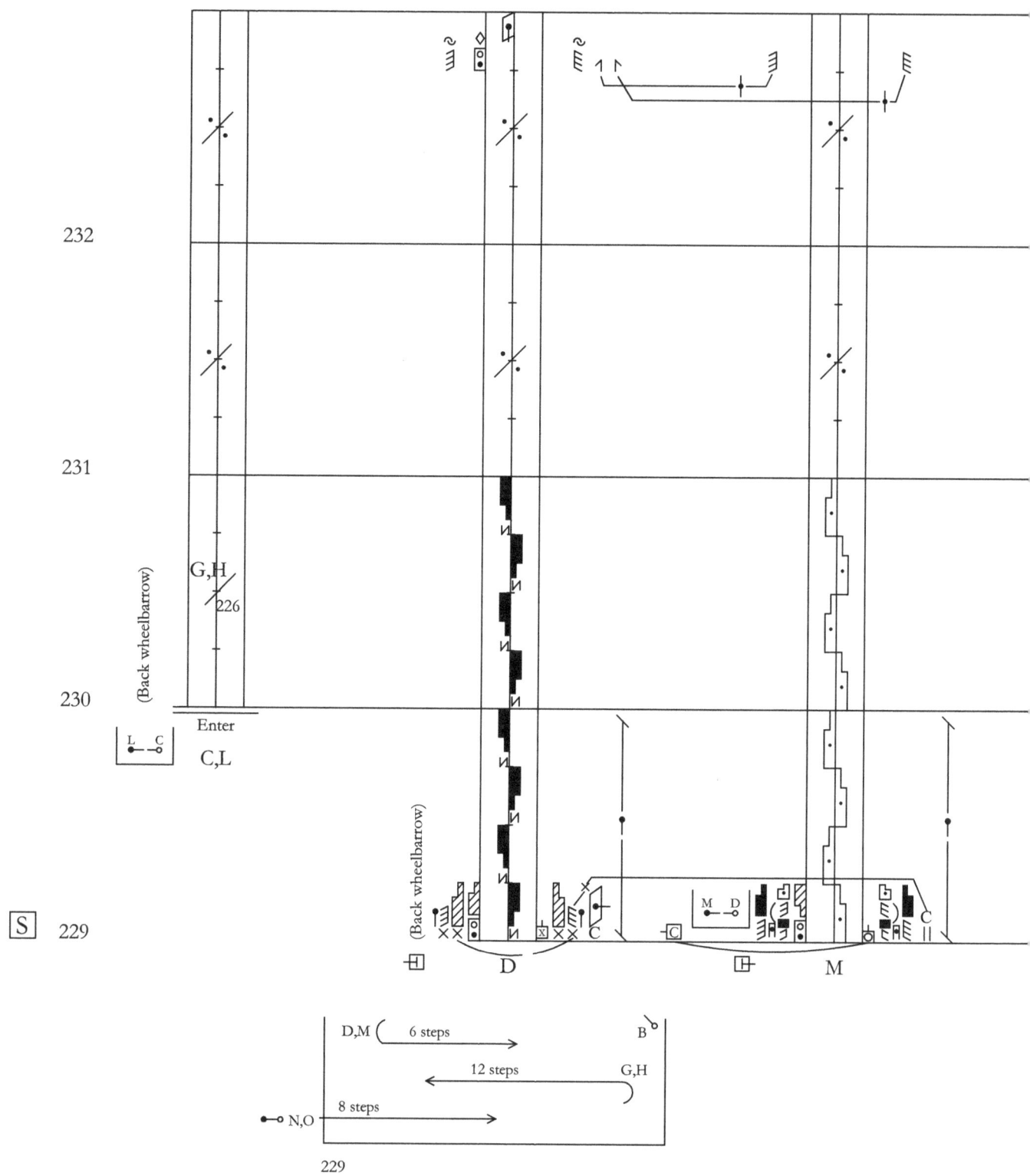

THE DANCE SCORE

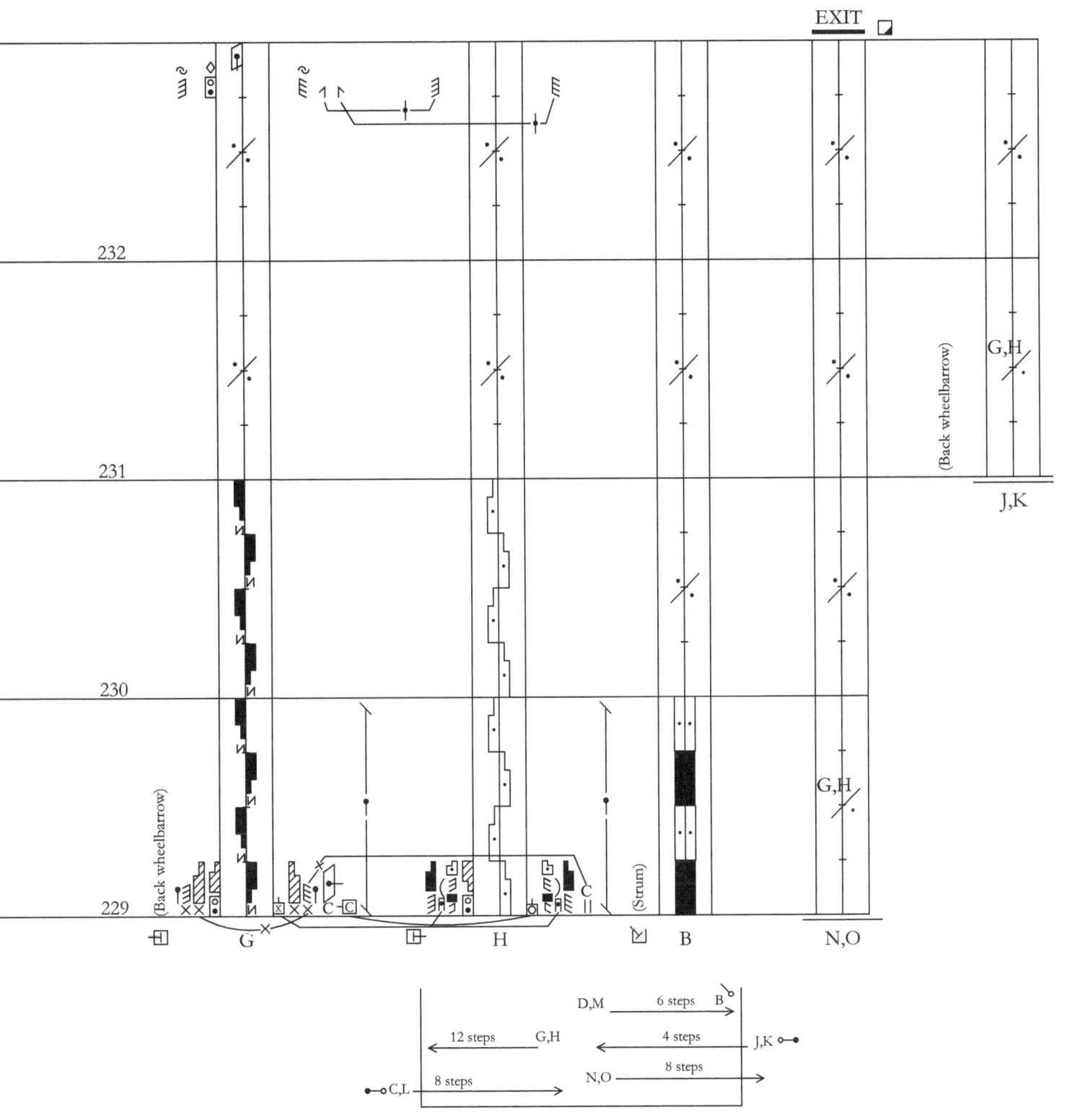

60 THE CHARLESTON BALLET

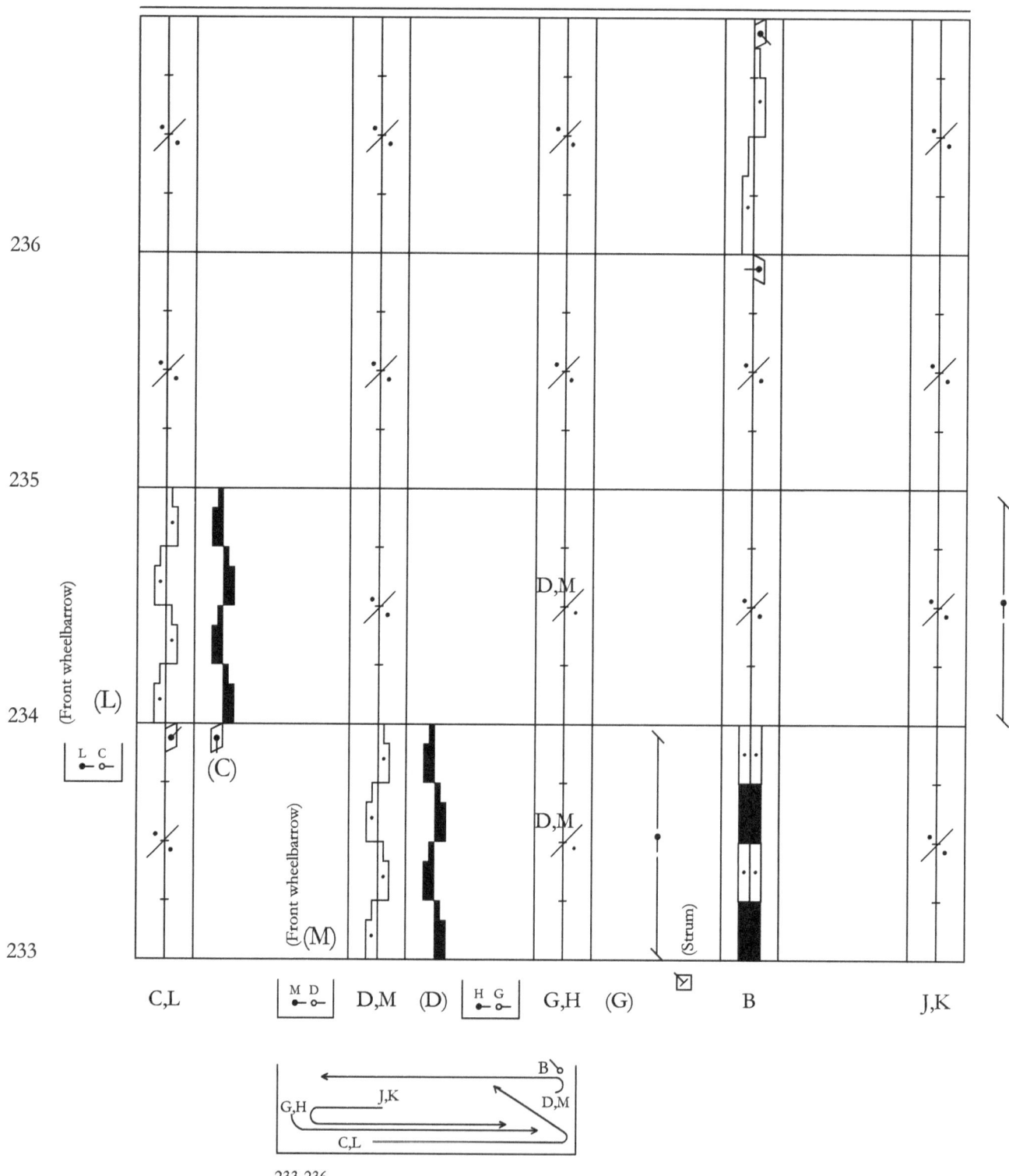

THE DANCE SCORE 61

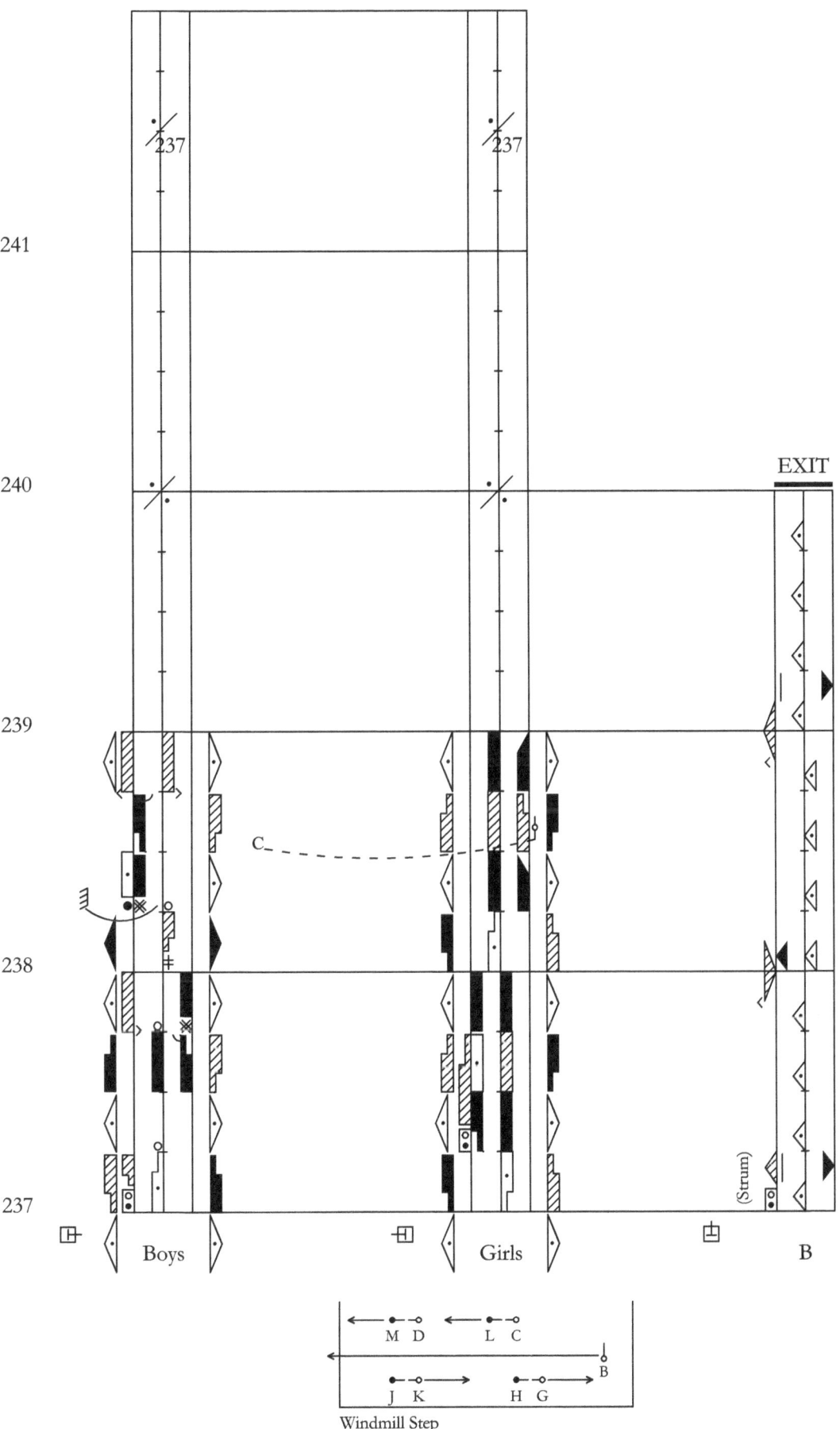

Windmill Step

62 THE CHARLESTON BALLET

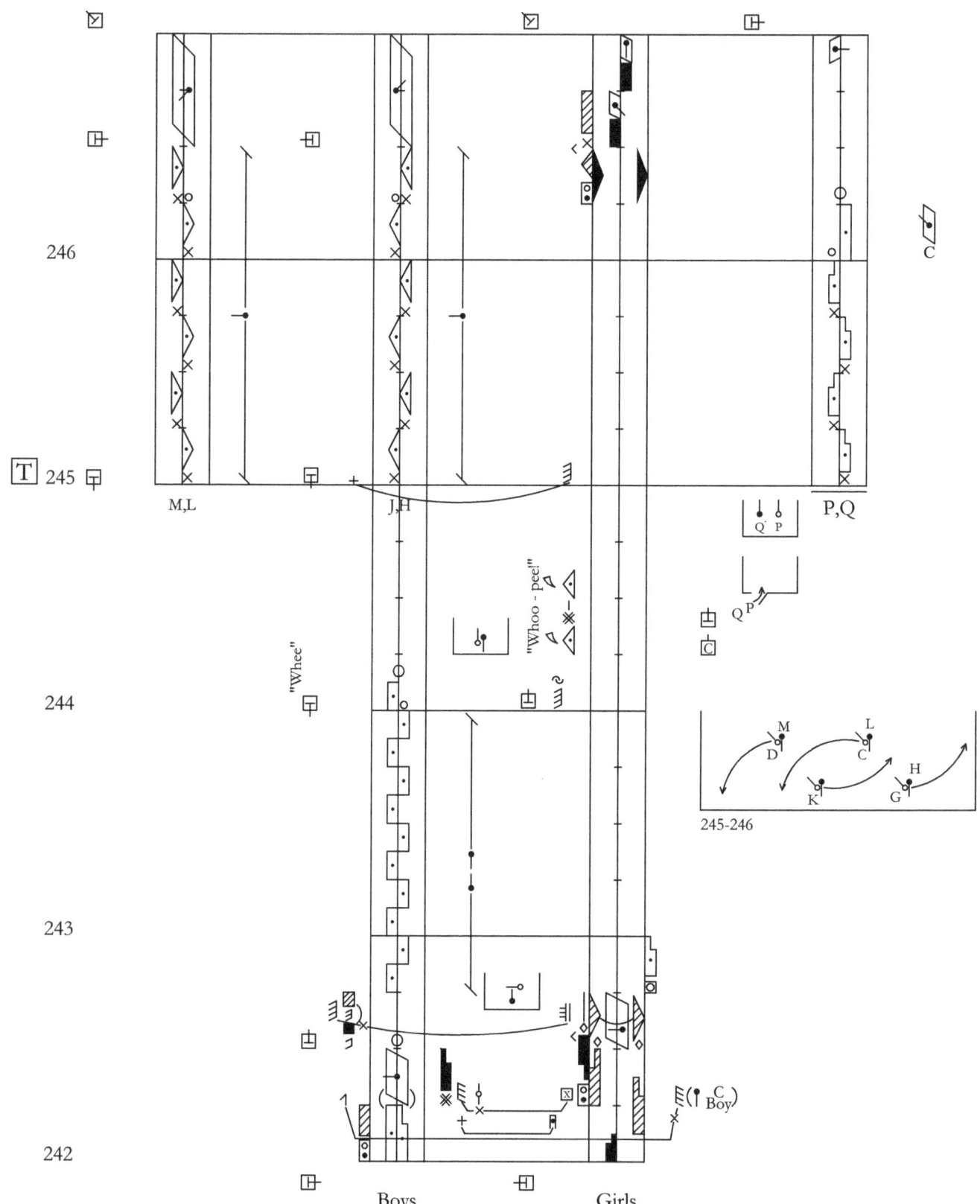

245-246

THE DANCE SCORE

63

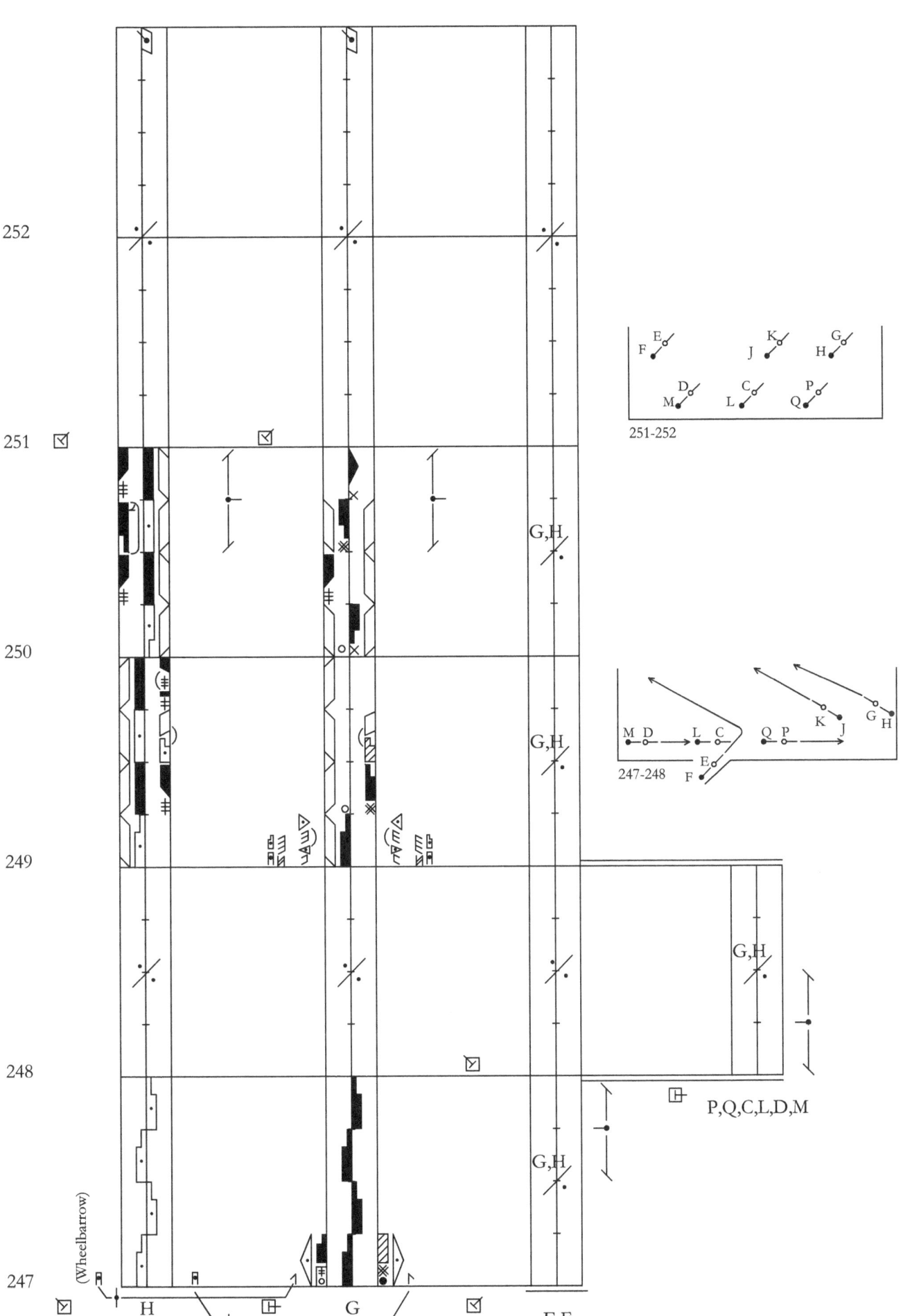

64 THE CHARLESTON BALLET

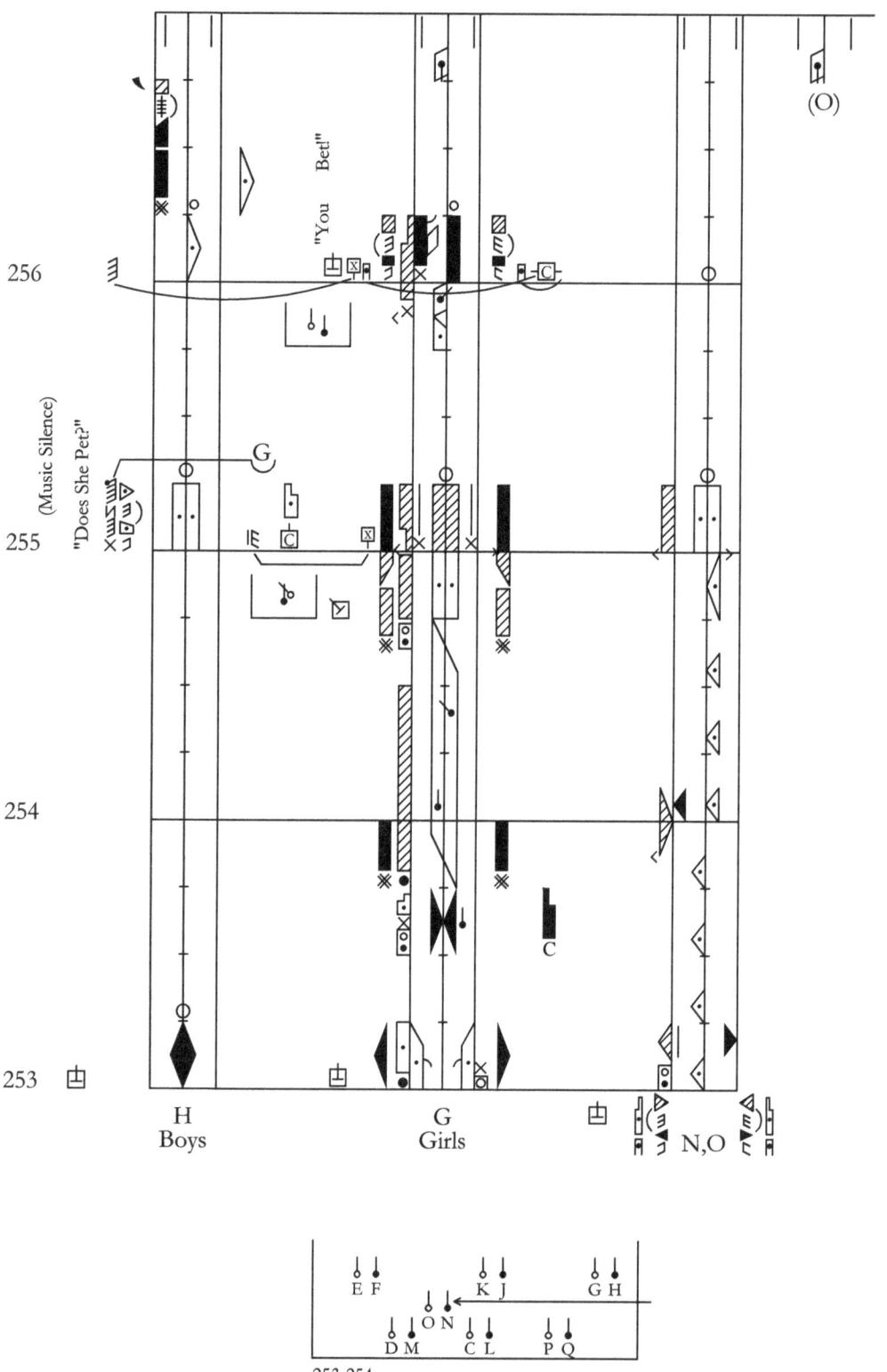

THE DANCE SCORE

65

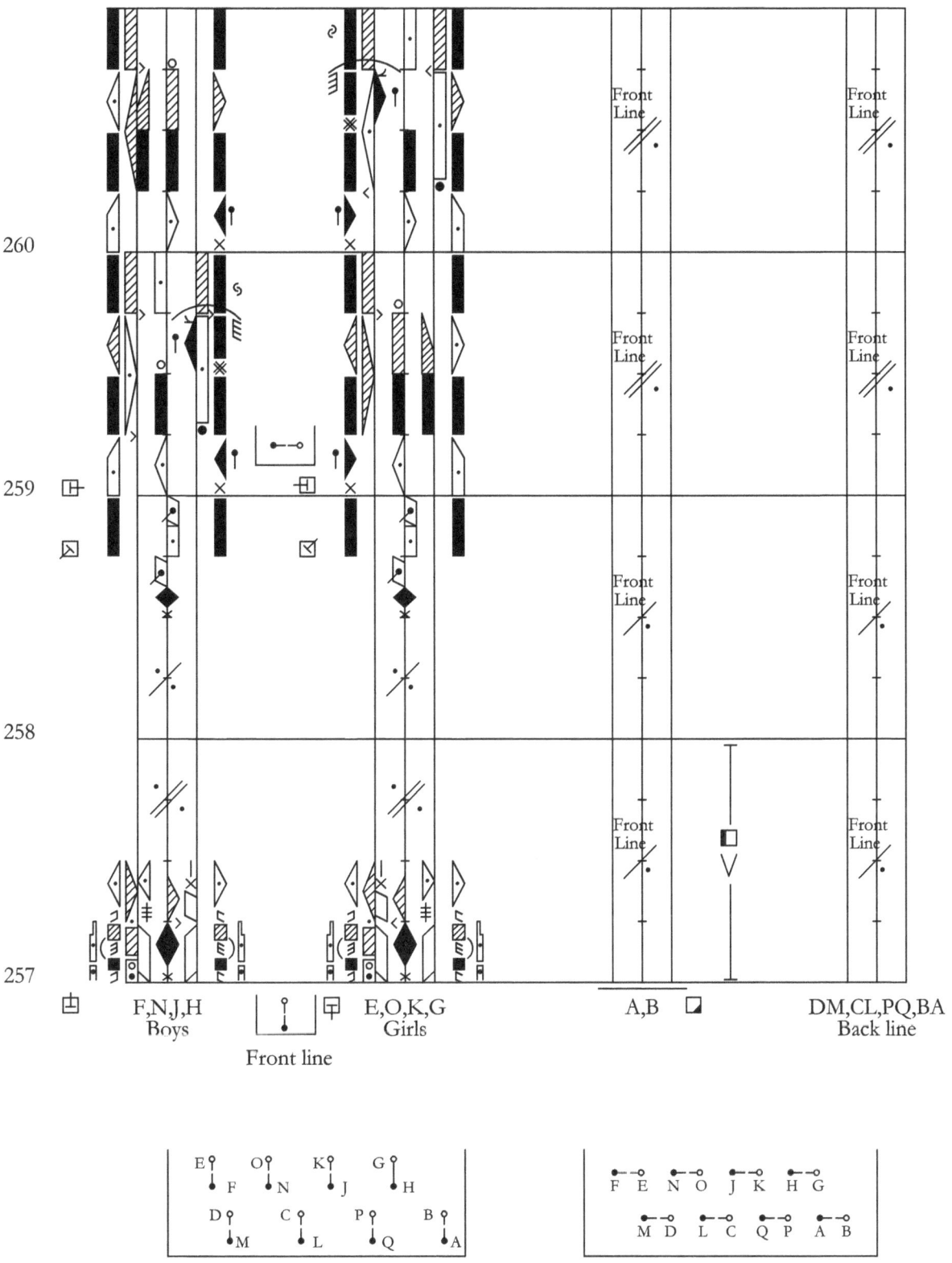

66 THE CHARLESTON BALLET

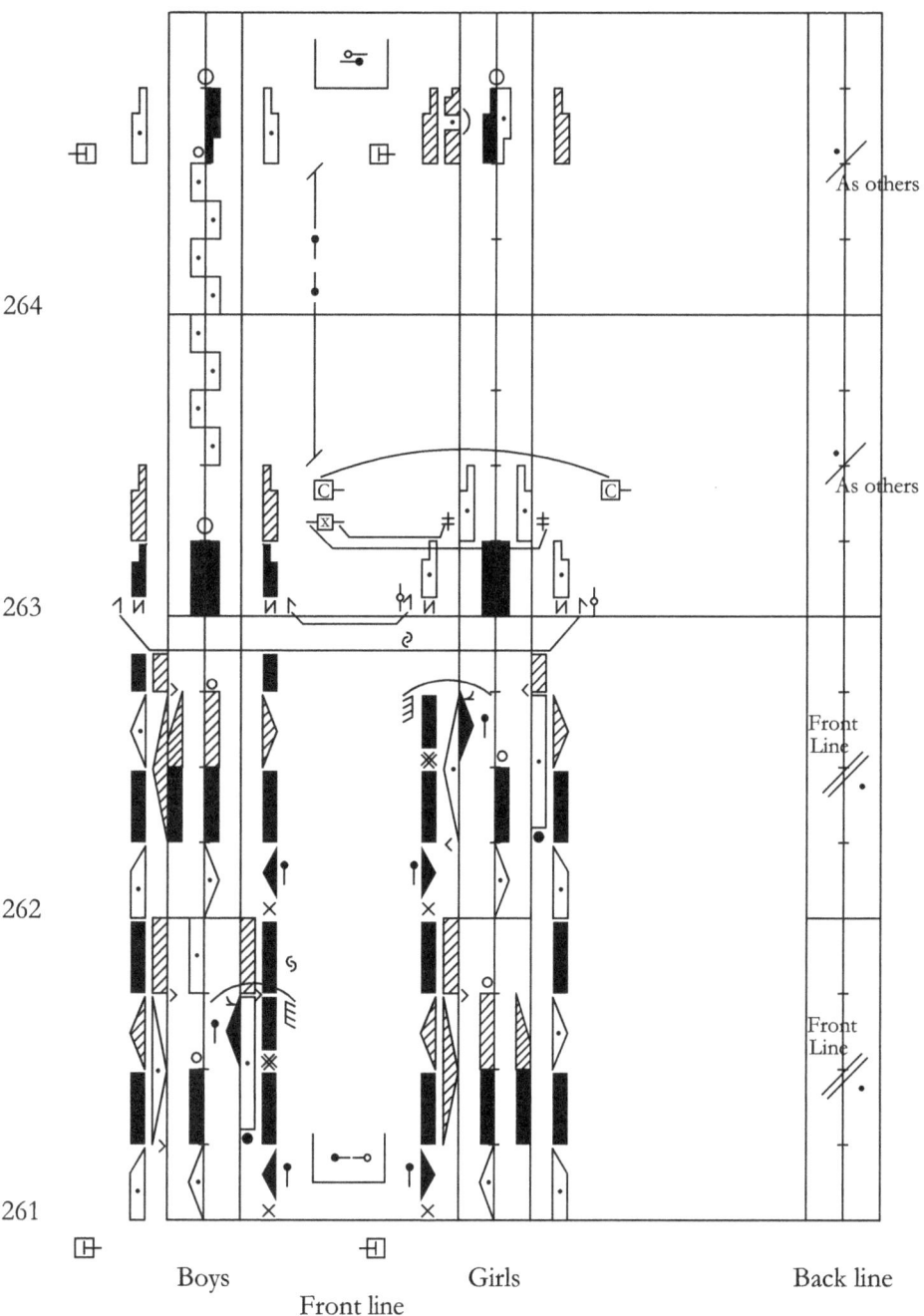

THE DANCE SCORE

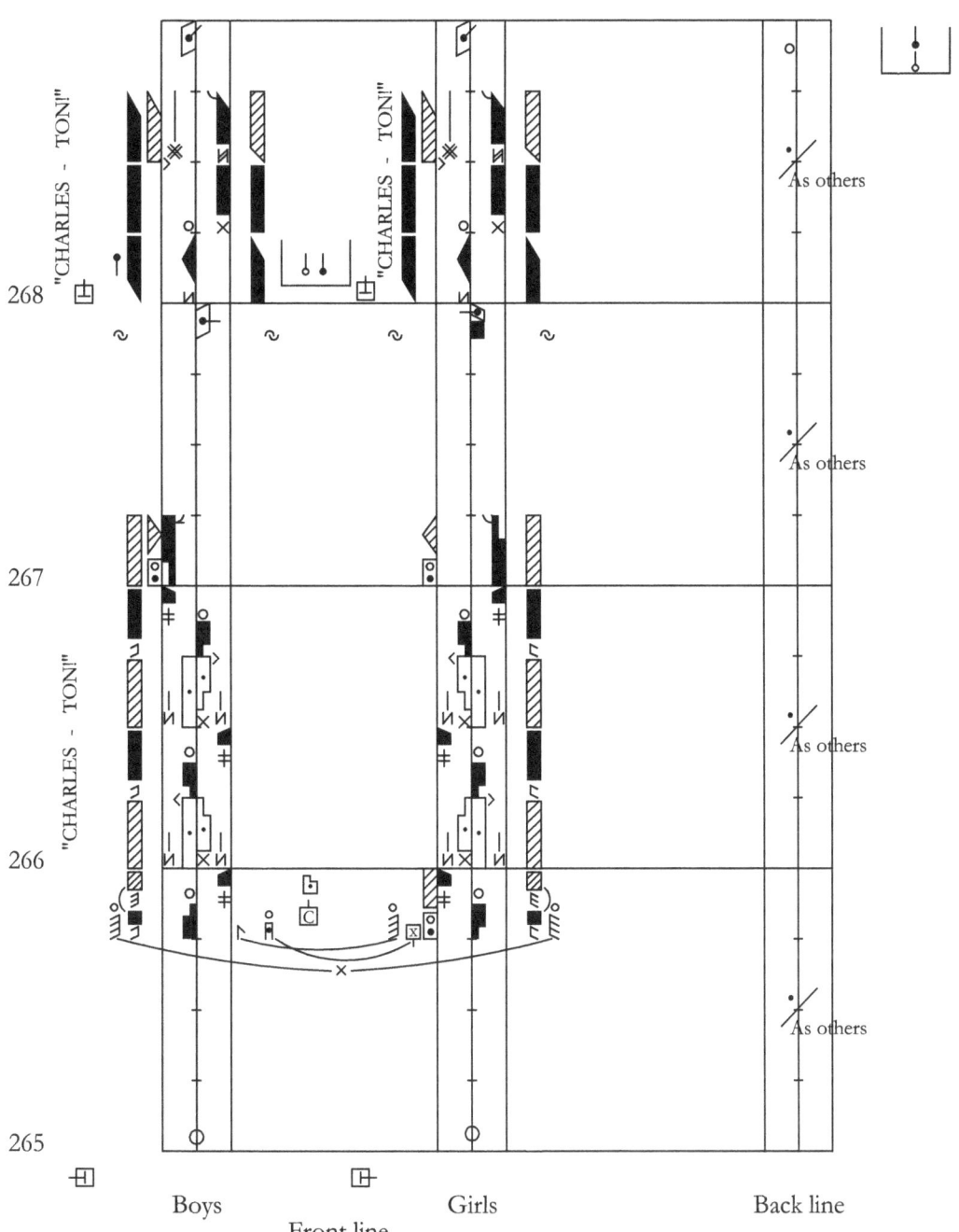

68 THE CHARLESTON BALLET

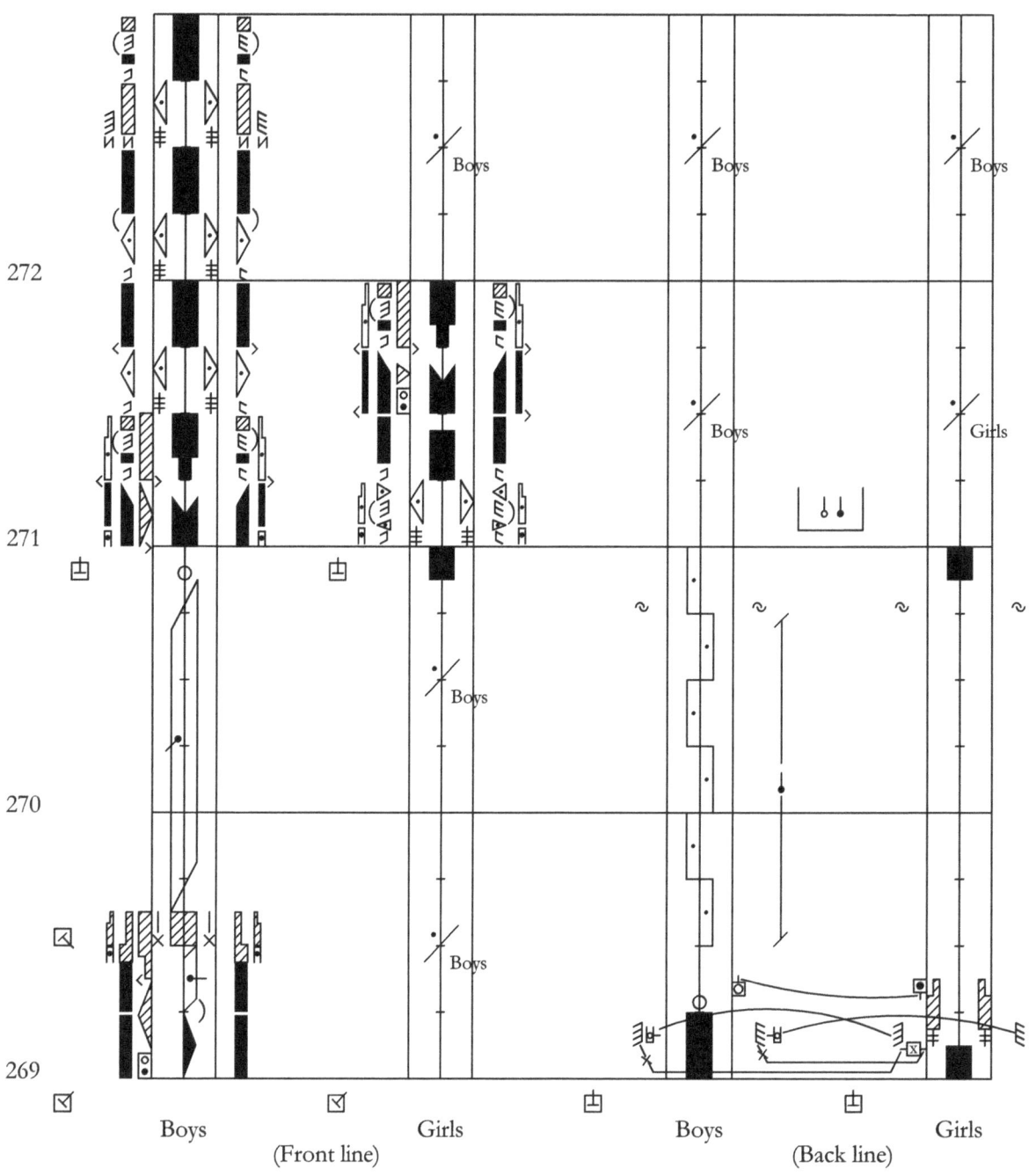

THE DANCE SCORE 69

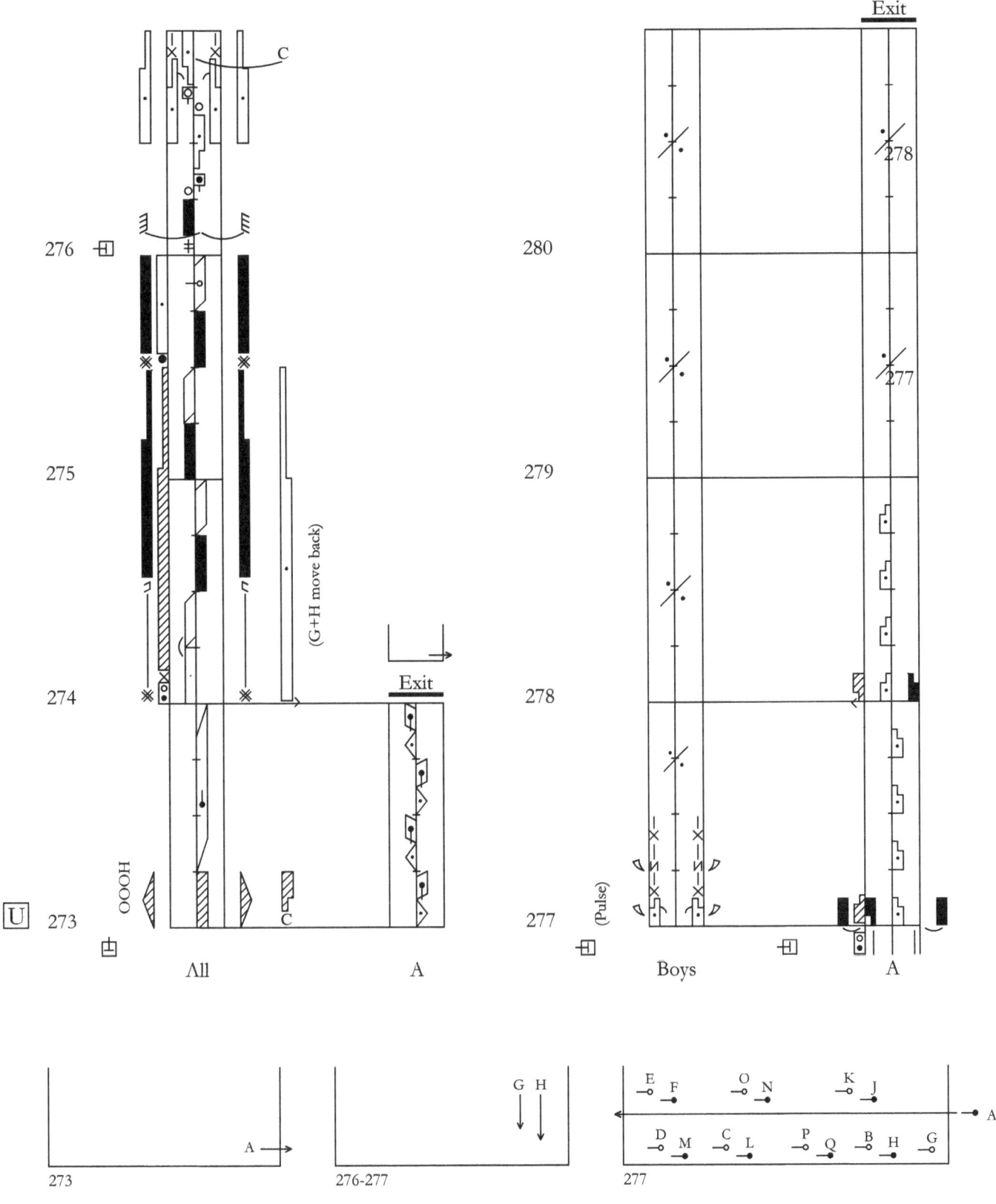

70 THE CHARLESTON BALLET

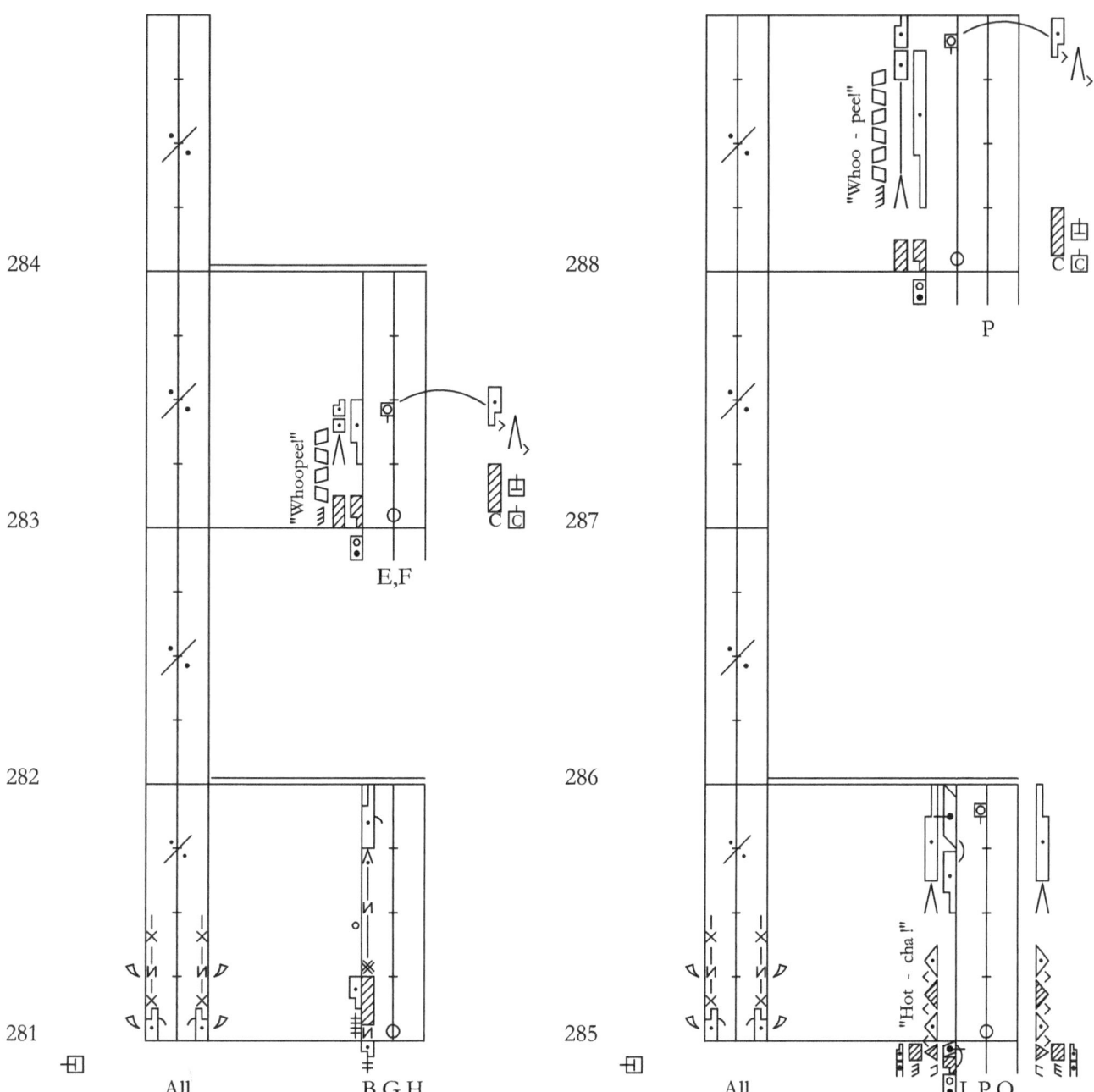

THE DANCE SCORE

71

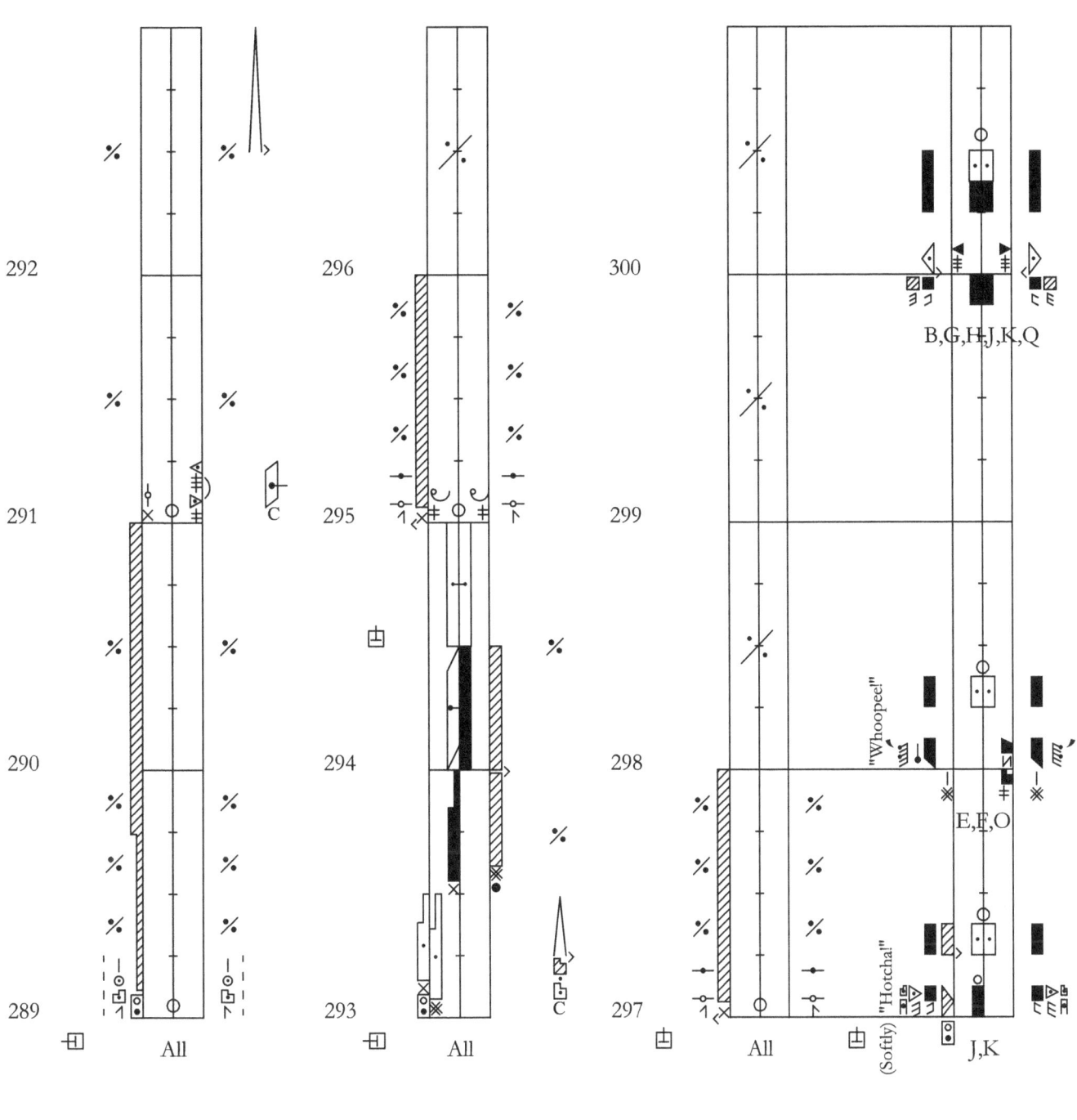

72 THE CHARLESTON BALLET

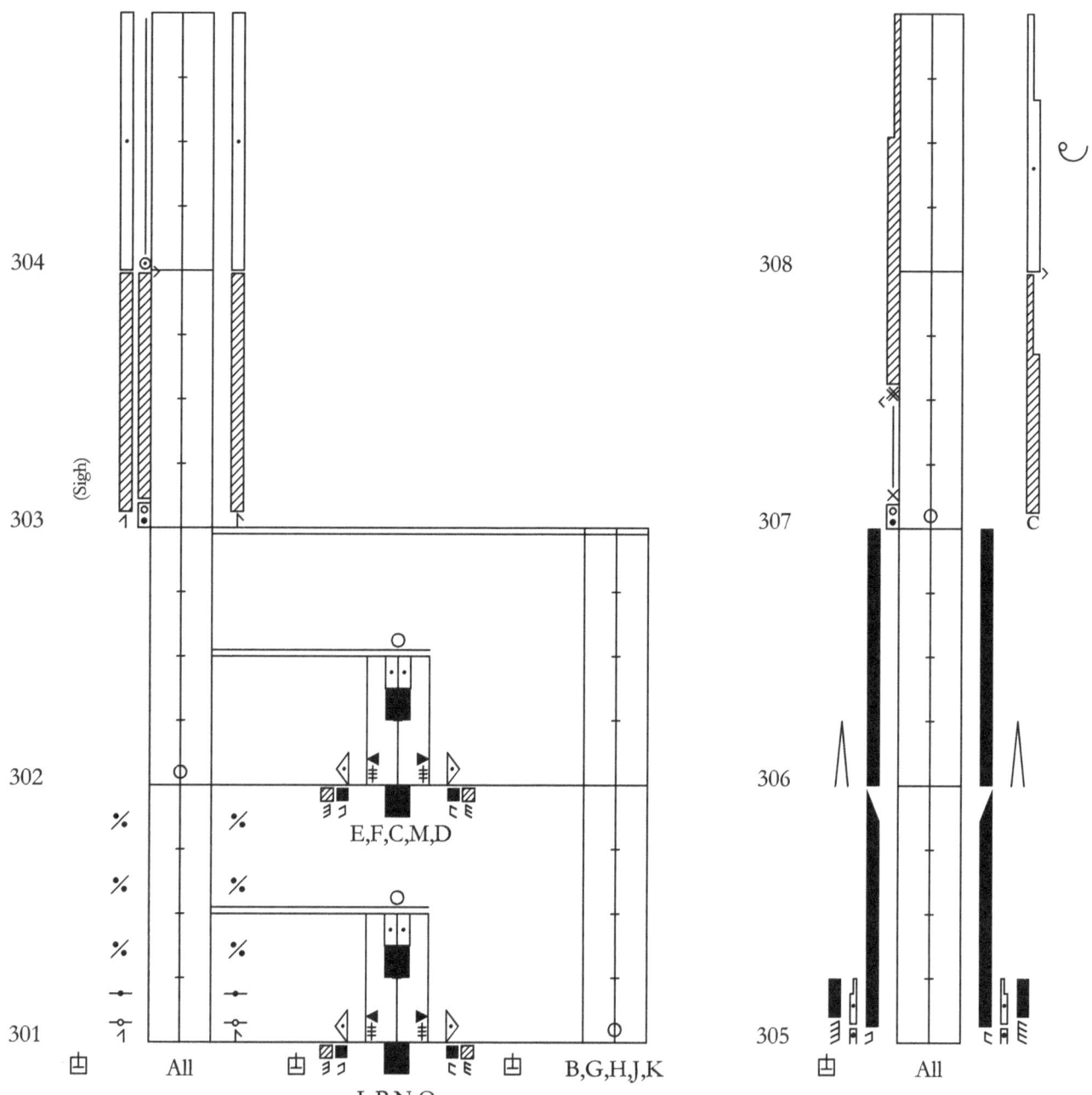

THE DANCE SCORE

73

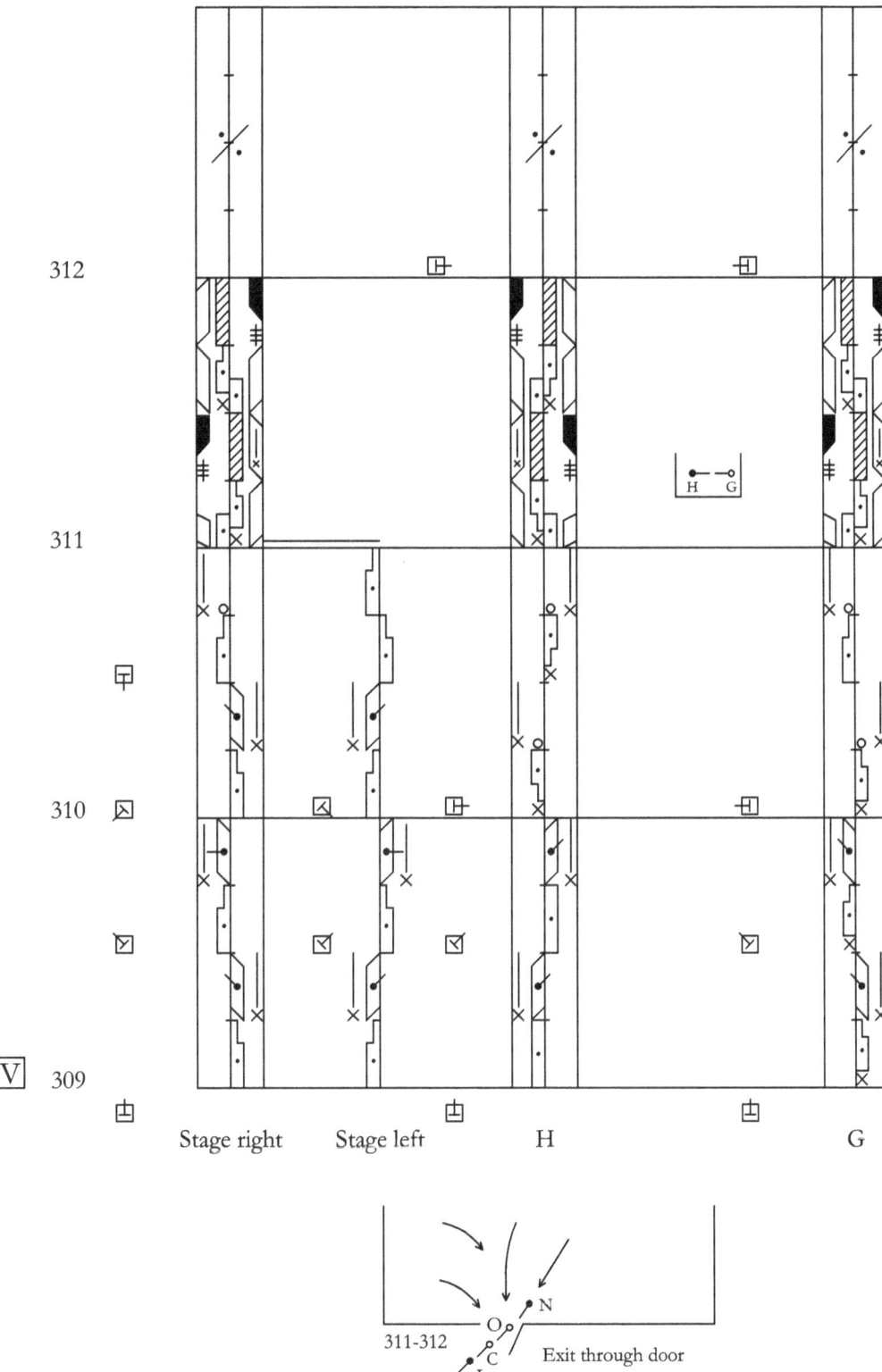

74 THE CHARLESTON BALLET

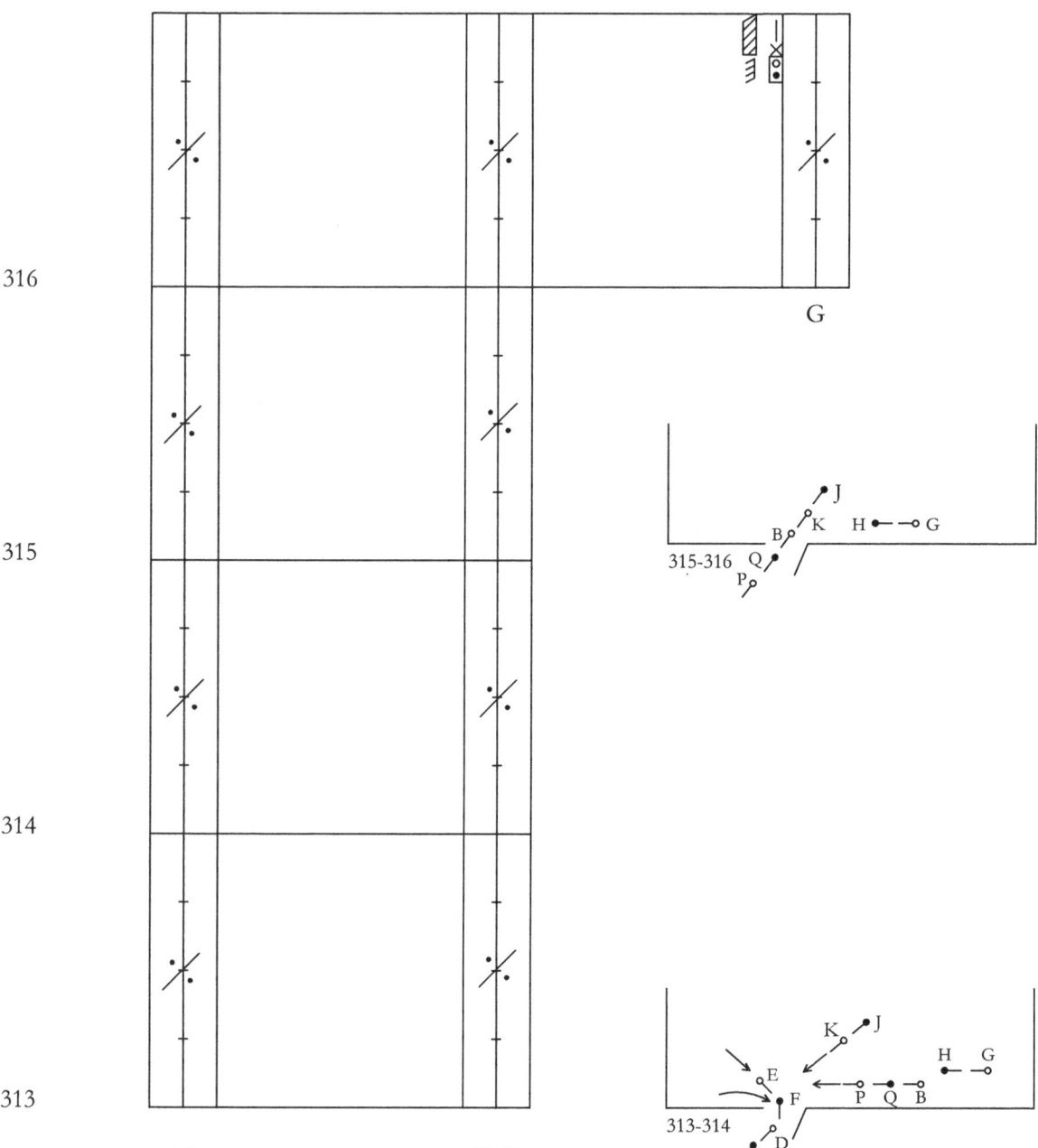

THE DANCE SCORE

75

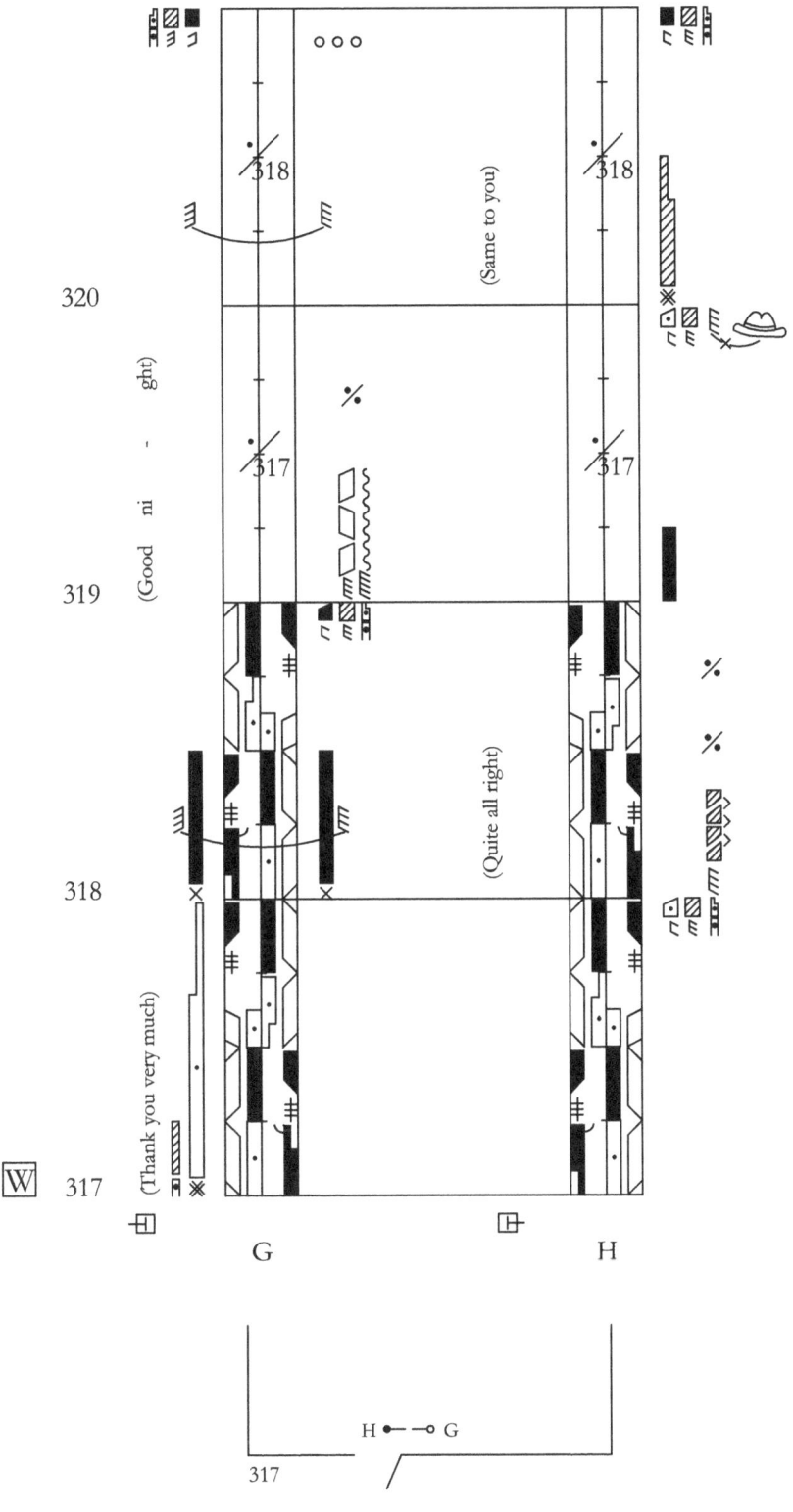

76 THE CHARLESTON BALLET

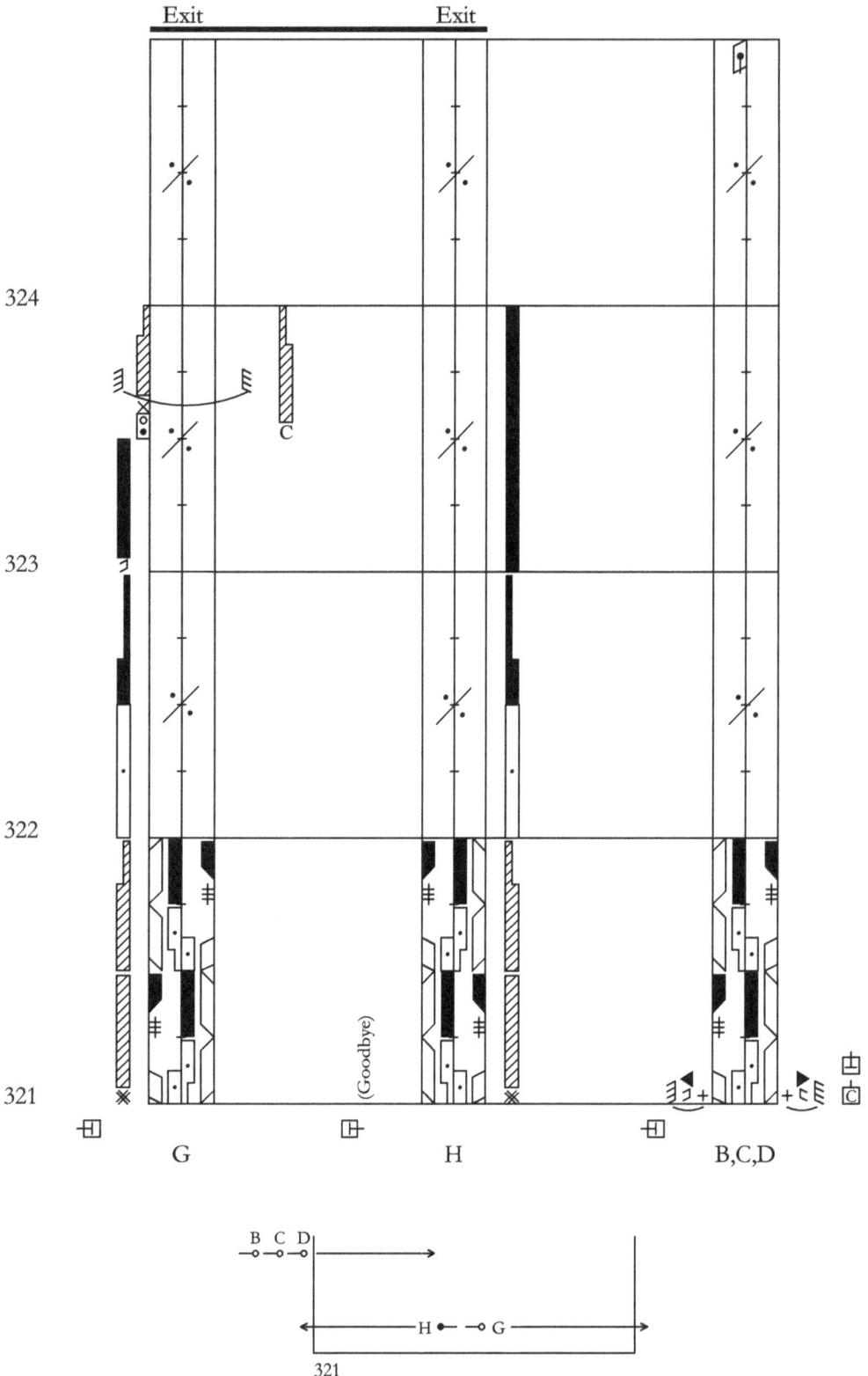

THE DANCE SCORE

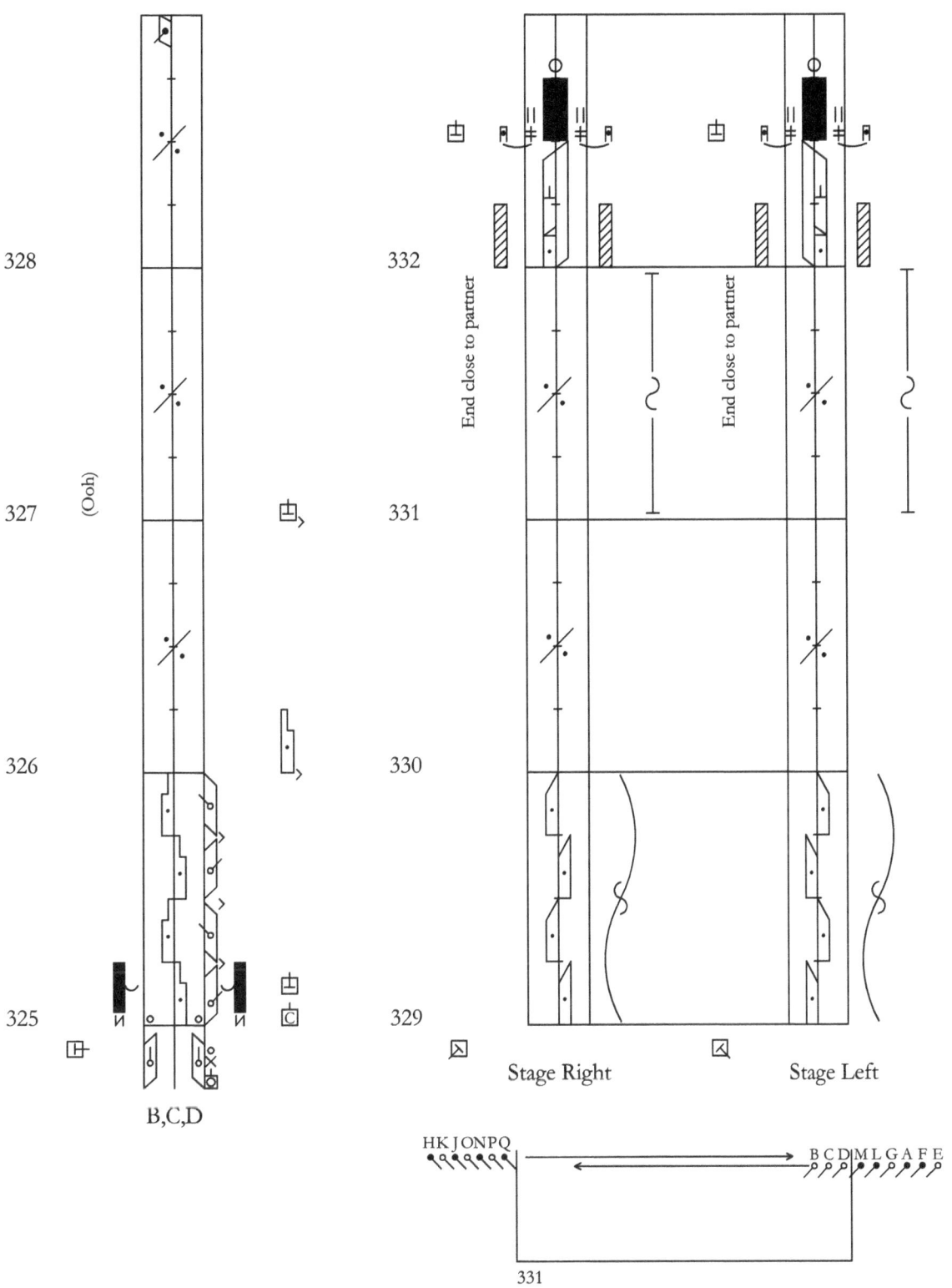

THE CHARLESTON BALLET

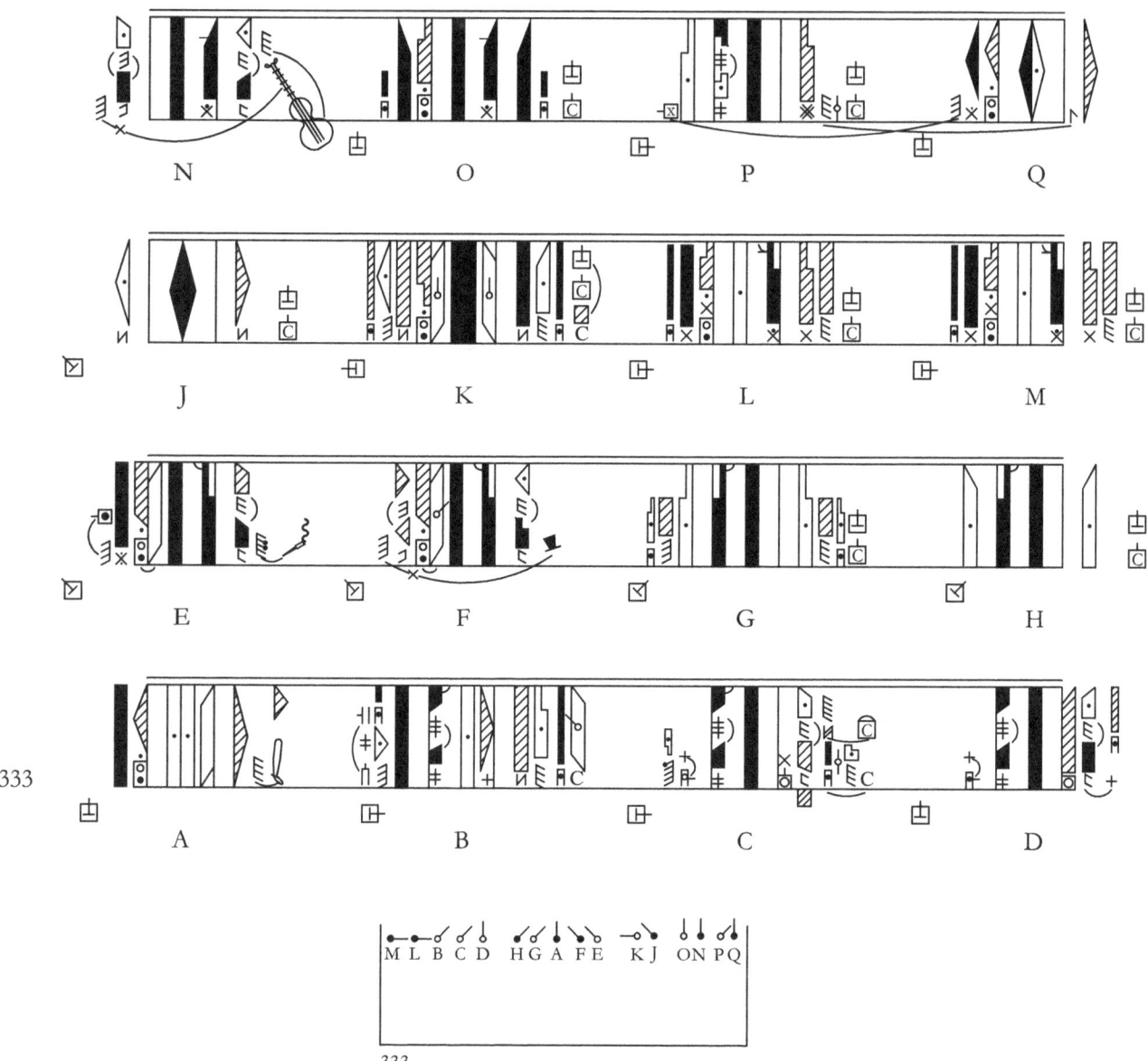

333

THE MUSIC SCORE

Music Copyright © 1945 Morton Gould

Rich Couple: Music Clarification. In the available videos of the Charleston Ballet, the measures of 61 to 70 have been cut. On meas. 71 and 72 the couple enter with the Charleston travelling step. Meas. 73 picks up on what is in the dance score.

THE CHARLESTON BALLET

THE MUSIC SCORE

THE CHARLESTON BALLET

THE MUSIC SCORE 83

84 THE CHARLESTON BALLET

THE MUSIC SCORE

THE CHARLESTON BALLET

THE MUSIC SCORE

THE MUSIC SCORE

91

92 THE CHARLESTON BALLET

THE MUSIC SCORE
93

PICTURES OF SPECIFIC MOMENTS IN THE BALLET

1. Measure 14, Flappers snooty

2. Measure 17, Flappers annoyed

3. Measure 19, Flappers Haaa!

4. Measure 39, Snooty expression

5. Measure 75, Rich couple, he knocks on door

6. Measure 78, Rich couple facing front

7. Measure 83, Timid girl, entrance

8. Measure 88, Good Time Charlie, You scared me!

9. Measure 91, Who, me in there, never!

10. Measure 99, Collegiate couple entrance

11. Measure 116, Collegiate leaning away

12. Measure 126, Timid girl pulled into Speakeasy

PICTURES OF SPECIFIC MOMENTS IN THE BALLET

13. Measure 127, Timid girl hanging onto door

14. Measure 128, Gangsters entrance

15. Measure 138, Gangsters leap frog

16. Measure 172, Juniors marking time

17. Measure 187, Old couple. You're a red hot Hot Mamma!

18. Measure 190, Old couple, he knee pattern, she thumb licking

102   THE CHARLESTON BALLET

19. Measure 192, Old man slaps her bottom

20. Measure 211, Timid Girl, hips wiggling

21. Measure 211 (end), Stopping hips; screaming

22. Measure 213, Timid Girl wild Charleston

23. Measure 221, Lindy with Charlie

24. Measure 244, Group airplane lift, Wheee!

PICTURES OF SPECIFIC MOMENTS IN THE BALLET

25. Measure 259, Over head kick

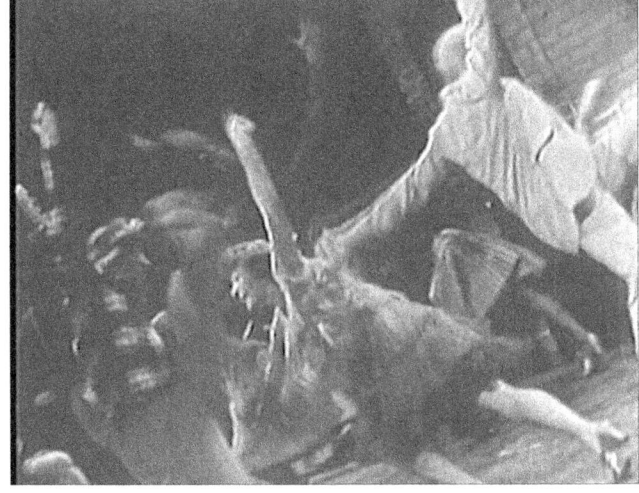
26. Measure 260, Angle shot

27. Measure 272, After two Charlestons!

28. Measure 277, Collapsed on floor

29. Measure 285, Hotcha!

30. Measure 295, Group exhausted

31. Measure 305, There it is!

32. Measure 308, Limp

33. Measure 317, Goodbye Charlie

34. Measure 319, It was very nice, Charlie

Measure 333, Final pose

Additional pictures

Measure 82, Timid Girl

Measure 122, Collegiate Couple

Measure 212, Timid Girl

Measure 249, Group

www.ingramcontent.com/pod-product-compliance
Lightning Source LLC
Chambersburg PA
CBHW081120080526
44587CB00021B/3682